TO EVERYTHING ITS SEASON

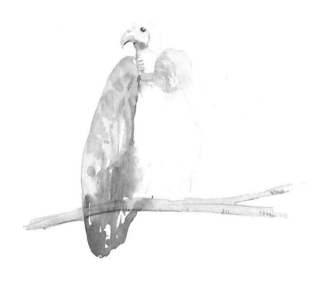

Gillian Rattray

TO EVERYTHING ITS SEASON

MalaMala
The Story of a Game Reserve

JONATHAN BALL PUBLISHERS

JOHANNESBURG

©Gillian Rattray

First published in 1986 by
Jonathan Ball Publishers (Pty) Ltd
PO Box 548
Bergvlei 2012

ISBN 0 86850 125 5

Design and phototypesetting by Book Productions, Pretoria
Reproduction by Lithotechnik, Pretoria
Printed and bound by National Book Printers, Goodwood, Cape

For my son David

To every thing there is a season, and a time to every
purpose under the heaven.

Ecclesiastes III, 1

ACKNOWLEDGEMENTS

I am extremely grateful to Mike and Norma Rattray for entrusting me with the delightful (though daunting) task of writing a book about their beloved MalaMala. A whole new world suddenly opened up for me: a world not only of animals, insects, flowers and trees, but of people: young and old, black and white, hunters and conservationists. Each of these I see as threads in a colourful tapestry, threads which I have endeavoured to weave faithfully into a fabric which I hope will do justice to this unique place.

Many people provided me with historical information. I thank them all, and in particular would like to mention: Harry Kirkman (with whom I spent happy hours visiting his old haunts in the Sabi-Sand Wildtuin); Len Grice (whose prodigious and precious memories of the early Campbell years he so generously shared with me); Mrs M Bodenstein; Esmé Lownds (who kindly lent me the manuscript of her unpublished memoirs); Dr Hamish Campbell (Wac's nephew); Mrs Toni Campbell (Urban's widow), and her son Athol Campbell; Colin Rattray (who was a fund of information on the Rattray family, particularly on his brother Loring); Nan Trollip; Tayi Mhlaba; and the staff of both the Killie Campbell Museum in Durban and the Africana Library in Johannesburg.

For the loan of photographs which I have used in the book, I thank: Mr and Mrs John Briscoe, (for allowing me to publish the photograph of Mrs Briscoe's father, Alec Logan, with Princess Alice and her lion); Dennis Cleaver; Hamish Campbell; Len Grice; Esmé Lownds; Colin Rattray; Norma Rattray; and the Africana Museum and Library and the Killie Campbell Museum.

During my frequent trips to MalaMala I was made to feel most welcome by the staff, who helped me in so many different ways. My

A pair of White-fronted bee-eaters sitting in their favourite spot — on a dry branch of a tree on the flood-plane of the Sand river.

son David organized my visits to the camp with kindness and efficiency and was always a willing provider of information. I am greatly indebted to him and to my daughter-in-law Nicky, for having me in their home, and for being so tolerant of the stacks of reference books, painting equipment, plant material and sundry creepy-crawlies with which I littered their dear little house.

I cannot adequately thank the MalaMala rangers for giving me so much of their time, sharing their knowledge, and for the fun we had. The quality of these enthusiastic and well-informed young men is outstanding, and is, I believe, what contributes greatly to the magic of MalaMala. Without the assistance of ranger Alan Fogarty, who waded into murky pools, climbed trees, and went far beyond the bounds of duty in assisting me in the collection and identification of botanical specimens, it would have been difficult, if not impossible, for me to compile the natural history sections of this book. I am deeply grateful to him.

My sincere thanks go to Yvette Hill, who, out of the goodness of her very kind heart, typed my manuscript for me so stoically and efficiently.

Finally, I thank my husband Peter for his advice, support and enthusiasm, and his cheerful forbearance in playing second fiddle, for the past eighteen months, to MalaMala.

Bauhinia galpinii ~ Pride-of-De Kaap; flowering in Elephant Alley on Toulon.

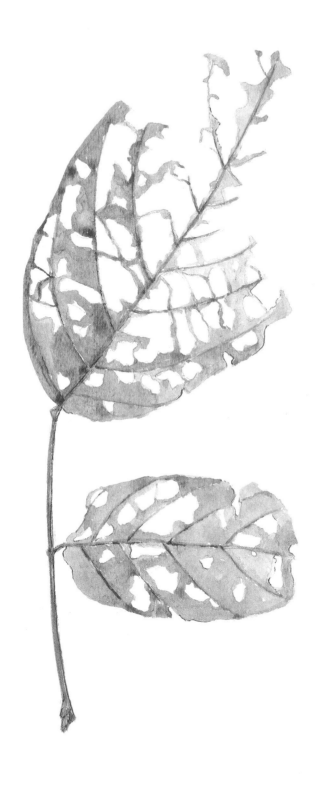

A much-enjoyed leaf I found
on the ground near the river.

MALAMALA – WINTER

…Winter slumbering in the open air,
Wears on his face a dream of Spring!
Work without Hope   Samuel Taylor Coleridge

The flight south from Phalaborwa brings us over the western area of the Kruger Park – a flat carpet of seemingly endless bush, the grey and sandy-beige broken only here and there as a stream threads its green-banked way through the level ground. Most of the waterways appear to be only beds of sand, and flow from west to east, finding their way easily from the high range of the Drakensberg mountains to the sea in far-off Moçambique. There is a sameness about the terrain which appears, from our height of eight thousand feet, to be unbroken by any geographical landmarks.

Now the Sand river comes into view, flowing at first in an easterly direction; as it turns southwards we can see quite clearly the sandy stretch where the Mlowathi stream joins it from the north. That is where Wac Campbell had his first MalaMala camp. A splash of colour, a cluster of thatched roofs, and we see for the first time the beautifully positioned present camp at MalaMala. Underneath us now is the MalaMala airstrip, the letters marked by a circle of white stones. Further south we fly, still following the path of the river; over the small grey cottages of Flockfield, then Beaumont's camp, then Charleston and then, as the Sand river bends once more eastwards, the neat green patches of lawn and painted green roofs of the quaint Victorian buildings of Kirkman's Kamp. This was once the TCL ranger's home; here Harry Kirkman lived, for whom the camp was named when Mike Rattray bought the farm Toulon from the Roche family in 1983.

1

Long-horn beetle
(Litopus latipes)

Colotis evenina ♂ ~ Orange Tip.

Beneath us the Sand river flows into the wider Sabi; the banks are greener, and the midday sun reflects on the wider expanse of water. A maze of buildings comes into view – the large settlement of the village adjoining Skukuza camp in the Kruger Park. We can see the bridge spanning the Sabi river, where the drift used to be. This is where the old rascal Steinacker built his blockhouse during the Boer War, which became the first home of Colonel Stevenson-Hamilton (he who turned everything upside down).

The wheels of our aircraft lower like the joints of some giant insect; we bank in a wide circle. Now there is no longer a sameness about the bush: the trees are varied in size, shape and colour; some quite leafless in their winter garb. Game-paths wind through the bush like the thin strands of a giant cobweb. We bank over a dirt road. I think of 'Skukuza' riding over to have lunch and perhaps a game of tennis at Toulon, with Crosby or Tomlinson. The giant trees of the Combretum bush loom even larger now. Then we're down, tearing along the tarmac runway which is edged with tawny grass and the dry flower stems of Wild foxgloves (Ceratotheca triloba). Beyond the high security fence is the bush, the same bush that was known by the Bushmen, and Louis Trichardt and Fitzpatrick and his Jock, and Kirkman, and Campbell…

The plane halts, and from the sophisticated technical twentieth-century interior of one world, we step down into the warm slightly fragrant air of another. A smiling ranger with tan-coloured tabs and 'RR' on his khaki shoulders steps forward. Our MalaMala adventure has begun.

Kirk, the genial Shangaan driver, welcomes us aboard his bus, and we drive through a small portion of the Kruger Park until we reach a high gate. While Kirk puts his signature to a permit, we read on a large board that we are now entering the private territory of the Sabi Sand Wildtuin. The gateman's kraal has a stout reed fence surrounding it; the latter is festooned with the inmates' cooking utensils. Not only does the vegetation tell us that this is Africa!

We drive parallel to the old Selati line. Stone ballast is all that remains since the line in this area was discontinued in the fifties because of the threat to game. I notice the small rise in the ground on the left where the

Grey-headed bush shrike

old Toulon siding used to be. What adventures began there! I picture the Varty and Unger children disembarking from the old steam train, exhausted from their long journey from Johannesburg, clambering on to Kirkman's old buckboard and setting off for Sparta on a winter's morning. And the Campbell hunters in the early days, before the pont was built across the Sabi, their arrival complicated by the enormous retinue of servants, dogs, horses, provisions and guns.

The tall appleblaar trees (Lonchocarpus capassa) still have their green leaves, while the round-leafed kiaats (Pterocarpus rotundifolius) are hanging on to the last of their yellow ones. Near the turn-off to Harry's Huts, Kirk halts the bus and points out some baboon to us. On the right the small blue cross of Maloney's grave shows up clearly in the short grass – the iron fence which Harry Kirkman erected around it fifty years ago stands rusting and neglected. Three warthogs are on their knees, digging for roots to the right of the road. Kirk slows down the bus so that all the passengers can see them. A little further on are the great mounds of the cattle graves – sad monuments to the years when disease proved so much greater than man.

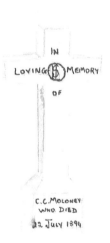

IN
LOVING MEMORY
OF

C.C. MOLONEY
WHO DIED
22 JULY 1894

Maloney's grave ~ a sad little monument at the side of the old Selati line.

Kirk has had a message on his radio that we should look out for lion at this spot as two lionesses and a lion were seen in the vicinity earlier in the day. We stop – and in the distance, to the south of the cattle graves we can just make out the outline of the three great cats lying in the shade of a tree. Those of us who have binoculars can see the animals more clearly. All three appear to be asleep. Unable to drive off the road, we leave the lions and move on.

A party of giraffe comes into view, and they glide elegantly across the road ahead of us. Kirk stops the bus and some of the guests press forward to take photographs. On the move again we dip down and up through a steep gully, along which, in Kirkman's time, great herds of sable antelope passed each afternoon on their way to drink at the river to the right. Our road follows the track the Shangaans made years ago, as their oxen dragged laden sledges. Tomlinson and Kirkman rode along the beaten track on their way to supervise the dipping of the TCL cattle on the farm 'Shaws'. Wac came this way, at first on horseback, and later in his truck the 'Queen Mary'; the poor young Arthur, in 1926, rode here, nervous and alone to summon help at Toulon. All the hunters in the years past came this way, their excitement mounting at the prospect of a month's shooting, men's company, camp fires, yarns and companionship. And in the later years, hundreds of visitors have traversed this narrow dirt road, cameras at the ready, just as excited as we are now.

We see a herd of impala ewes, and there is another burst of chatter and clicking of cameras. I see Kirk smiling, thinking to himself, no doubt, that many more impala will be seen.

The camp - Malamala.

Through the bus window I watch a pair of Bataleur eagles soar high in the bleached midday sky, and as we swing round the bend past the Princess Alice bush, I know we are seeing everything just as it was when the old highveld farmers came here each winter with their sheep and their guns and their sharpened knives. And then we drive under the boom, and the Shangaan man, with rather serious demeanour, salutes smartly, and we ride over the neatly-swept gravel in front of his guard hut. Then through another dip, and there is the bougainvillea. And like the guest who recalled her visits of the thirties, at the sight of the bright creepers which have been a glory at MalaMala camp for the past fifty years, my heart too turns over.

There is something very special about arriving at the thatched reception building at MalaMala. Perhaps it is the smiling faces of bronzed, khaki-clad rangers, who stand in a row to meet us, introduce themselves informally, and step forward to carry our bags; perhaps it is the pleasure of walking along the swept gravel paths flanked by neatly kept grass; or the brilliance of the pink and white Impala lilies which flower so surprisingly from bare grey stems; perhaps it is the tantalizing glimpse of the river beyond the thatched terracotta bungalows; or the big trees; or the screech of the Glossy starlings busy in the bare marula trees; or the plaintive 'go-away' call of the ubiquitous Grey loerie, which is almost the signature tune of the bushveld. Perhaps it is all of these. And after unpacking in the cool, informally elegant rooms which smell wonderfully of thatch and are so shiningly clean, there is lunch in the pleasant dining room, watching through the wide windows, the birds dropping down from the old ebony tree like falling leaves, to feed on the crumbs scattered for them on the lawn. And the Sand river beyond. If you look ever so carefully you might see the quick movement of an animal slipping through the reeds to drink.

After lunch a drowsiness settles on the camp, the silence broken only

Bataleur eagle seen in flight.

5

Impala lily ~ Adenium multiflorum growing in the camp.

Young waterbuck

by the rhythmical swish of the paths, being raked and the birds calling. Few mad dogs and Englishmen in these parts! (I was once sitting at my window, painting, when I saw a Grey duiker step daintily from the bush and pass my room. I followed, talking quietly to it; the buck kept looking back at me, but seemed unafraid. I kept my distance, and trailed the animal as it stepped between the huts and then down towards the river. It was a magical moment, not witnessed by anyone else. I might have dreamt it, but for the little hoof-marks left in the newly-swept gravel paths).

At last it is tea time, taken on the wide verandah – tea, hot or iced, and home-made scones. The landrovers are already lined up outside reception; the black trackers sit on a long bench in the shade, chatting together as they wait for us.

Our ranger takes us to our vehicle, and we clamber in and settle ourselves on neatly-folded blankets. He slots a rifle into a rack in front of the dashboard. Someone makes a crack about the presence of the gun, but we are assured with a smile that it is there 'for real'. The ranger gives us instructions, to be silent when game is seen; not to stand up in the vehicle as the animals have become accustomed to the shape of the vehicle and may react if the shape is broken; not to throw cigarettes or litter into the bush, and to feel free to ask the ranger any questions. Then we are off on our first game drive. The ranger speaks into his radio which is connected both to the person at reception, and to all the other vehicles, informing them that we are on our way. The winter sun is warm on our backs, the air fresh on our faces.

Baboon lope off the road as we approach the boom where the 'guard' darts towards the road which our ranger indicates. We are saluted solemnly as we pass under the striped pole.

Tiny cream flowers hang like catkins

Colotis evenina – Dry season form.

Tiny cat·kin·like flowers hanging from some knob·thorn trees

Vervet monkeys – turning their dark
little faces towards us .....

from the tips of the branches of some knob-thorn trees (Acacia
nigrescens); mousebirds move in the leafless branches. We turn towards
the river, where the grass is thick and tawny and the bush fairly dense.
A bushbuck ram steps shyly from the cover, the sun dappling its strong
hindquarters. He is joined by two females, which we are told is fairly
uncommon – these buck are usually seen on their own. The male
bushbuck can be surprisingly aggressive, especially in the rutting
season, and have been known to fight to the death over a female. In a
bare-branched Acacia robusta tree vervet monkeys turn their dark little
faces towards us. An Emerald-spotted wood dove rises from the road
ahead of us, displaying the wonderful cinnamon of its tail feathers; it
settles in the road again having to repeat its take-off as we approach.
We cross the Sand river over a solid concrete causeway, which replaced
the sectioned wooden structure which Wac's pals at Natal Estates had
once made. Downstream a Pied kingfisher hovers over the water,
head down, looking for fish.

Our tracker signals with a low whistle, and we halt.
He points out three kudu cows with two young
females. Outside the rutting period, which has just
ended, the males tend to remain on their own or in
bachelor herds. As the kudu turn to stare at us,
the sun behind them turns their large ears
to red.

We come to a newly-made dam,
which the ranger tells us filled with
water which appeared only after bush in the area was cleared. Three
giraffe have just finished drinking – there are still wet patches on the
sandy dam wall. Now they are browsing on the fresh green leaves of an
acacia tree. We are told that the giraffe have some unique characteristics:
they are the tallest animals in the world; they have the longest gestation
period (457 days) of all ungulates; they walk by swinging their two legs
on one side in unison (quite unlike the horse); while having a long neck
enables the giraffe to eat leaves out of reach of other animals, unlike
other antelope, the giraffe can't scratch its head with its back legs.

7

Pied kingfisher – perched
above his favourite pool.

Discarded Masked weaver nests on a
bare marula tree at camp.

Dry Clematis brachiata ~ Traveller's Joy ~
festooning the bush near the Flockfield boma.

Dry legume species.

Dry flower-stalk of White Seringa ~
Kirkia acuminata. (A gift from Annie)

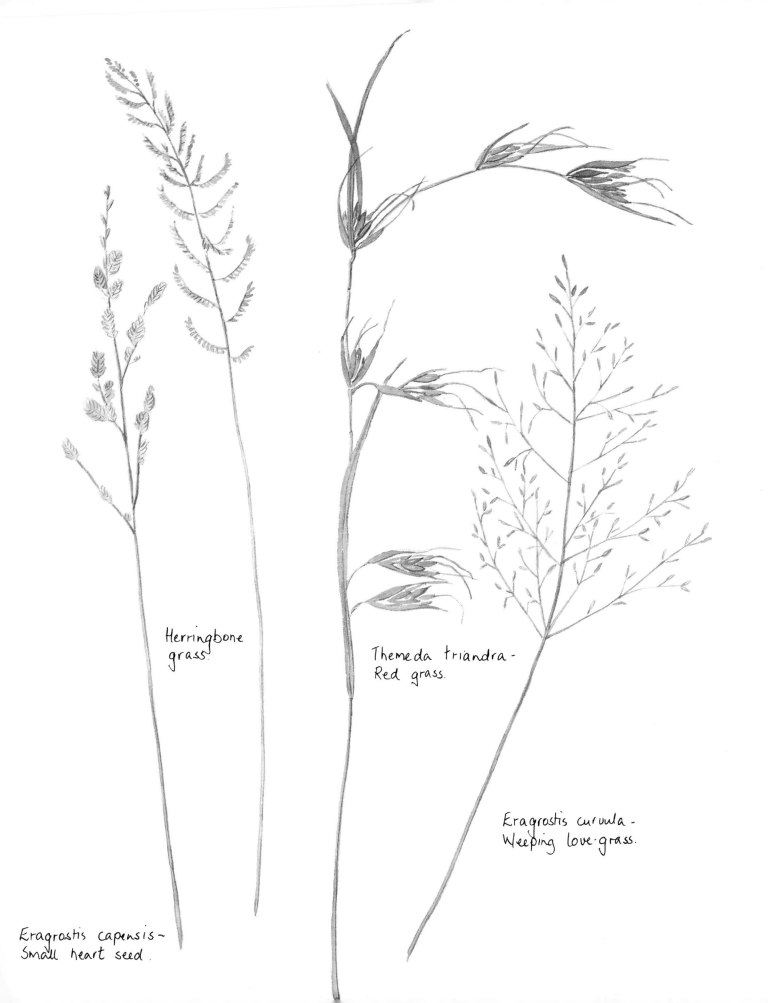

Herringbone
grass.

Themeda triandra -
Red grass.

Eragrostis curvula -
Weeping love grass.

Eragrostis capensis -
Small heart seed.

Red-billed oxpecker

Fork-tailed drongo ~ constant companion of the herbivores.

Nature, however, thinks of everything, and we see the solution to the giraffe's scratching problem in operation. Each animal is host to a number of Red-billed oxpeckers. These little birds, who cling to the animals skin, rather as a woodpecker clings to the bark of a tree, take care of the ticks and other parasites which feed on the blood of the animals. (It is said that an oxpecker can consume 7 000 ticks a day. How on earth would one count?) A Fork-tailed drongo, the constant companion of herbivores, sits above the animals in a tree; smart and sleekly black, the dapper little bird is ready to dart down from his perch to snatch at insects as the antelopes' hooves disturb the grass. In the bushveld wherever there are animals grazing, there will always be a drongo sitting in a nearby tree.

We take the road to the left of Campbell koppies, and drive through the area which in Campbell's time was a sanctuary. Long-tailed shrikes fly into a marula tree. We stop to look through our binoculars at the large rather untidy nest of a White-back vulture, high in the fork of a giant leadwood tree (Combretum imberbe). This species of tree is the slowest-growing and also the oldest tree in the bushveld; some specimens which have been carbon dated have proved to be thousands of years old. The wood is immensely hard, which makes the trees almost indestructable; most of the standing dead trees in the bushveld

White-backed vulture leaving its nest in a giant leadwood tree.

are leadwood trees. The wood from the trees makes excellent firewood. It was used exclusively by the hunters of old, who would light a fire at the commencement of camp, and it would burn continuously until the winter camp ended. In the boma at MalaMala, the finely grained logs of the great fire come from these dead trees.

There is a great deal of fresh buffalo dung in the road, so we follow the spoor which leads us into a grassy area fairly thickly covered with dry Strychnos bush. We bump across the uneven veld, and come across an enormous herd of massive dark animals, which seems to stretch in every direction. Our ranger estimates that there are well nigh on two hundred Cape buffalo in the herd. The bulls are mostly on the perimeter, the cows and reddish brown calves in the centre. Some are lying down chewing the cud. They appear to be totally unconcerned at our arrival, although one large bull steps forward, nose outstretched, and glares at us in the way buffalo have, as if, someone once remarked, you owe them money! The bosses of his massive horns seem almost too heavy for his head, wrinkling the skin over his eyes. His centre parting and corrugated, slightly 'curly' look of the bosses are reminiscent of Oscar Wilde. Some of the huge beasts lumber to their feet, others continue to munch the Panicum grass. Our ranger says that despite their docile, almost domestic appearance buffaloes are regarded by hunters as the most dangerous of animals, becoming relentless and formidable attackers, particularly when wounded. Buffalo have only been seen at MalaMala within the last twenty years; the rinderpest epidemic of 1896 almost wiped them out, and subsequent outbreaks of foot-and-mouth disease further limited their numbers. Wac and his hunting pals never met the buffalo here. Perhaps as well for them. We leave the animals contentedly enjoying their evening graze.

The light is failing; the sky is beginning to turn lavender and pink. The bare trees are etched in marvellous silhouette against the western sky. Our ranger turns the vehicle on to an open area of veld, and we stop to have our evening drink. John, the tracker, erects a folding table, and prepares to heat our venison kebabs over a spirit stove. The ranger

Dry pods of Russet Bushwillow – Combretum Zeyheri.

11

Cape buffalo bull.

White rhino bull – facing us in the glare of the flashlight.

dispenses drinks from a coolbox. We stand in the cool evening air and watch the sun slip beneath the horizon, and count the stars as they appear. The trill of a Scops owl comes from a nearby thicket; an answering call echoes back.

Everyone dons jerseys, jackets and woolly caps. John switches on a powerful spotlight, and we begin our drive in the dark, which is so magical and exciting. The bush has quite a different feel at night: perhaps it is that we are isolated by the darkness, or perhaps it is that our senses of smell and hearing are heightened because of the blanket of the dark night, broken only by the sweeping arc of John's searchlight, and the yellow rays of the landrover's headlights. We are very quiet, and there is a strong sense of anticipation, which heightens as we overhear our ranger receiving radio instructions regarding the location of a lioness and her cubs.

A herd of impala is caught in the spotlight's beam – their eyes reflecting the light. They stand statue-still, heads turned towards us. 'Sitting ducks' one of our party whispers to his wife. Thank goodness, I think to myself, we're not hunters.

As we come around a bend in the road, a White-tailed mongoose scuttles to the front and the side of us. He stops once, caught in our beam of light, looks at us with his head up, then hurries away into the cover of the bush. These nocturnal animals, which are one of the largest of the mongoose family, live on insects, small rodents and frogs. A moment later John's flashlight picks up the unbelievably large grey mass of a rhinoceros, almost on the road. The animal's large and strangely flared ears flicker. It swings its massive body round and trots off into the bush. We follow, our vehicle taking the smallish bush in its stride. John somehow knows in which direction the animal has gone, and points the light where the driver must turn. We get another beautiful view of the great beast as he stands at the end of a clearing. He is apparently a lone bull. Rhino bulls are territorial, demarcating and defending their territory when necessary. We are told that last week a fight was witnessed between two bulls, the rather unusual outcome being the death of one of the animals, who was mortally wounded by his rival's

Winter sunset

horn. Although rhinos have poor eyesight, their sense of hearing is
acute, and the disproportionately large ears, quaintly fringed with hair,
can rotate independently of one another. The ranger explains that the
name 'white' rhino probably stems from the Afrikaans for the word
'wide' describing the square lip, which feature distinguishes our friend
from his irascible cousin, the so-called 'black' or hook-lipped rhino. The
white rhino has no incisors, and can use his great wide lips to good
effect in cropping the grass as short as if a good lawn-mower had been
over it. The ranger informs his colleagues of the location of the rhino,
and we bump across the veld, back onto the road, in search of lion.

In the distant darkness a light shines, and we know that we are almost
at the scene. Two other vehicles are already there, the occupants semi-
illuminated and ghostly-looking in the light of the vehicles. Everyone is
silent. We receive a half-whispered message from one of the rangers
from the other vehicles, instructing us how best to proceed. Padding
along the road in front of us, quite unconcerned at the stir she is causing,
is a large, sleek lioness, followed by three cubs. The babies turn
frequently to look at us, then trot on after their mother. One, more
playful than the others, runs up to his mama and boxes her tail with his
front paws. Perhaps they have been walking for some time, as the cubs
take the opportunity to lie down each time their mother pauses in her
purposeful walk. She is apparently out hunting. As silently as possible
we follow in the rear.

As we move slowly along, keeping our distance from the little party,
we see, shining in the light of the flashlight, the tiny stars of impala
eyes. The lioness has seen them too. She stiffens. The babies who are at
least a metre behind her freeze into little statues as their mother bounds
off like a flash after the buck. A few minutes later she returns, empty-
handed. She then moves off, looking very determined, to the left, and
although we noticed no communication between her and her offspring,
the cubs move off together to the right and disappear in the bush. Our
ranger turns the vehicle, moving back along the road, hoping to
intercept the kill, if there is to be one. There is no sound or movement
from the bush. The lights of the vehicle are turned off, and we sit in the

13

Arniocera erythropyga –
Fire Grid Burnet. The
bright colours indicate
that the insect is
distasteful to predators.

dark and wait. Ten minutes go by, and we turn round again and drive to the spot where we last saw the cubs. In the dark we wait again. After a few minutes John, (who with his finely-honed bush sense can feel something happening) turns on the spotlight, and we see the lioness walking back through the bush on our left to the exact place from where she departed. As she comes on to the road the three cubs rush from their hiding place and run to their mother's side. What an incredibly touching sight, and what a superb illustration of training and discipline.

We leave the little family together in the road, and drive off silently back to camp.

Whereas luncheon at MalaMala is heralded by the strange notes of a blown kudu horn, dinner is announced by the beating of drums by black maidens garbed in long, rich-red garments. In accordance with tradition laid down at Campbell's first camp, the evening meal at MalaMala is always served in the round, beautifully made, reed boma, where guests sit in a ring at small individual tables (which used in the old days to be paraffin boxes), encircling a huge fire of leadwood logs. Because it is winter, each guest is provided with a plaid rug which can be used either on the knees or shoulders. A spotlight placed strategically in the magnificent giant ebony tree gives a soft greenish glow to the scene; and a long buffet table stands laden with dishes of deliciously-smelling food. Waiters serve us with soup. (I wonder if, as in Campbell's time, the soup will be worthy of a verse – it is), and then we help ourselves to a variety of well-prepared dishes including, as always, MalaMala venison. We are sitting here under the same spreading tree in the boma where, since 1930, so many others have sat, swopping yarns, recalling the day's events, enjoying the magic of MalaMala.

My telephone rings at 6 am – the winter hour for waking for the morning game drive, which we shall go on after breakfast.

The sky is a washed-out cloudless blue, the winter air sharp and bracing; I am glad of my warm jacket, and of the sun which will soon be increasing in strength. We are in the first of the landrovers to leave,

Member of the order Hemiptera. The long mouthparts are adapted for piercing and sucking.

Lion cubs ~ their tummies tight as little drums.

which is exciting, as the spoor of the animals will be fresh on the roads.

The veld-manager has radioed into camp that he spotted a lioness disappearing into the bush just beyond the boom, and has left a branch in the road to indicate the position. We turn off the road into the bush at the marked spot. About 100 metres into the bush we see the lion party. There are two adult females and three fairly large cubs. Beside the tree under which they are lying is a partially-eaten carcass of a wildebeest, which must have been killed the previous night. We wonder if the cubs have also partaken of the wildebeest, as their tummies are as tight as little drums, and they seem to me to be uncomfortable, as they restlessly move from one spot to the other, only settling down for a minute or two. The largest cub, a male, is obviously the leader – where he goes the others follow. They make mewing sort of growls. The mother and aunt take no notice of the youngsters, or of us, for that matter, the only movement either of them makes is to yawn and flick an ear. It is a very charming and peaceful domestic scene.

We turn back on to the road and head for the river. A Brown-headed parrot sits in a bare-leafed marula tree. On the old airstrip a party of warthog potter about – two are on their knees rooting in the short grass with their hard noses. A large female (we know her sex as she has only one pair of warts just below her eyes) stands squarely on and looks at us, before turning tail and trotting off. As the whole party moves off their ridiculous tails rise vertically as if at the press of a switch. The adults have long reddish manes reaching right down their back – the hair is

Brown-headed parrot.

Mr and Mrs warthog making off in a hurry – flags held high.

While the ranger peered beneath the bonnet of our land-rover I looked back towards the airstrip. This is what I saw.

Kalanchoe rotundifolia.

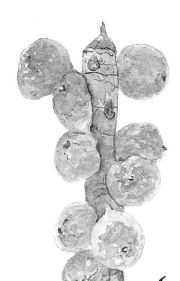

Dry crassula flowerhead.

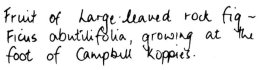

Fruit of large-leaved rock fig - Ficus abutilifolia, growing at the foot of Campbell Koppies.

Crested francolin

Ripe pods of the Scented-thorn acacia ~
Acacia nilotica. Both leaves and pods of
this tree are relished by game.

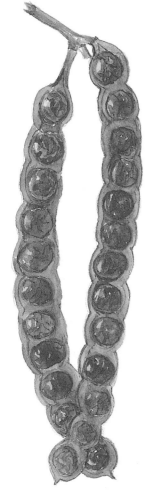

Dry fruit of Buffalo thorn ~
Ziziphus mucronata.

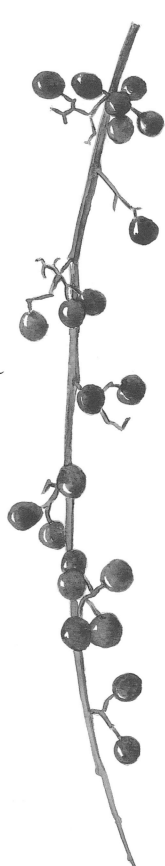

Cetoniid beetle

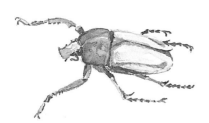

Swainson's francolin : usually found near streams and waterholes.

caught by the breeze as they run from us, but even this redeeming feature does little to detract from their overall comical appearance. Five waterbuck pause to gaze at us, and then move off slowly, the stately male bearing his large horns with great dignity. We are told that the waterbuck in this area are renowned for the length of their horns. In fact in 1931 Mr Jack Campbell (no relation to Wac) hunting at MalaMala bagged the world record for the length of horns of a waterbuck $37^{1}/_{16}$ inches (94.25 centimetres).

A pair of Swainson's francolin, dark brown with red faces, fly off from in front of the vehicle. These francolin are active in the early morning and in the evening, lying up during the heat of the day. African Monarch butterflies flit slowly across our path; their orange colouring and leisurely flight are indications that they are generally distasteful to predators, which may stem from the fact that their main foodplant is the poisonous milkweed (Asclepiad).

African monarch

We cross the river at the West Street waterhole, and take the road which runs parallel to the dry bed of the Matshaphiri river. (This is where Alec Logan despatched Old Two-Toes the lion in 1951). On our left there is a crashing in the bush, and John says confidently: 'Ndhlovu' (elephant). A huge bull is having his morning feed. We reverse into the bush and get a good view of him as he stuffs the broken leafy branches into his mouth with his versatile and supple trunk. He is none too pleased at being disturbed and makes what our ranger says is a 'mock'

18

Lone bull elephant — making mock charges, giving us all a fright.

Female leopard sitting at the base of a termite mound.

charge, but seems real enough
to me! The old giant is in fact not too
serious in his attempt to get us to remove ourselves – he takes only a few
menacing paces forward, ears outstretched. At the end of his short
charge, he tosses a small leafy twig into the air, almost like flinging
down the gauntlet. After everyone has taken pictures, we leave the old
boy to his morning meal. Elephants consume about 200 kilograms of
food daily, and have, our ranger informs us, a rather incomplete
digestive system; but this is all part of nature's plan, and the indigested
food provides nourishment for all manner of tiny creatures. The
elephant, we hear, is second only to man as a modifier of the
environment.

While we stop to examine a dead leadwood tree, our tracker whispers:
'Ingwe' (leopard). With breaths held we look where his finger is
pointing. Wonderfully camouflaged, a female leopard lies at the foot of
a large termite mound in the dappled shade of the bush. She raises her
head and stares at us with her deep yellow eyes. We are only a few paces
from her. It is difficult to describe the encounter. In her eyes there is a
timelessness, and a belonging; her ancestors have been in this place for
aeons of time, until evolution wrought the final miracle of lithe, sleek,
efficient cat which we see before us. She is perfection, and she meets our
gaze, as it were, on her own terms. No one dares speak. After a little
while the ranger talks quietly into his radio, informing others of the
location of the leopard. Otherwise there is silence, but for the shrill cries
of a flock of parrots who fly noisily overhead.

The leopard rises, stretches and moves slowly to the other side of the
anthill. We follow as quietly as possible. She appears unconcerned. Two
vehicles join us, each filled with guests who look eager and intent. The
leopard sits again, staring at us in a way which leaves no doubt that we
are intruders. Finally she walks slowly through the bush and climbs on
to the antheap where she settles in the shade of a large leadwood tree.
Her movements are reminiscent of water flowing, so supple is she. Her
coat is a beautiful gold, dappled with regular dark rosettes and spots
which stretch down to her toes. Her markings which we can see are

19

Colotis antevippe ♂
Red Tip. Dry season form.

such an effective camouflage are hers alone – no two animals are identically patterned.

As we drive around the furthest side of the antheap, we see that from one of the lateral branches of the overhanging leadwood tree, the carcass of a Blue duiker hangs. One of its rear legs anchors the dead animal to the branch; its head and forelegs dangle loosely. Part of one haunch has been eaten. The leopard, obviously replete after her meal of duiker, which she has skillfully removed from the reach of any predators, stretches out on her antheap, closes her eyes, and sleeps.

We turn southward towards Buffalo pans, where the thick tambotie trees have lost their once red and yellow leaves. The dry pods of an Asclepiad creeper festoon an Acacia tortilis (haak-en-steek) with the silken white cotton of their seeds. I notice a hornet's nest cleverly constructed in the grey dry branch of a silver-leafed Terminalia tree. Close by a praying mantis has laid her eggs on a dry thorn bush. The white case, which feels spongy, is made in a remarkable way. The female exudes a liquid which turns to foam as it comes into contact with the air. Before the foam hardens, she shapes it with the end of her abdomen, and fashions a series of little compartments, into each of which she deposits an egg. A tiny valve at the top of each compartment allows the hatching mantis to escape. What a mind-boggling construction.

A Yellow-footed bush squirrel darts up a tree at our approach, wisely making for the further side of the tree's trunk.
At Buffalo pans, two kudu are browsing on a dry Red bush willow tree (Combretum apiculatum). What was grey mud in the summer has hardened now into concrete-like crusty fissures. There are baboon droppings in the road. We see some of these animals in the bush to the right of us. One old baboon, perhaps the head of the troop squats beneath a tree and eyes us

Duiker carcass cleverly suspended from a branch of a leadwood tree.

Yellow-footed bush squirrel.

Egg-nest of Praying mantis on Acacia nilotica

warily. We are now in knob-thorn-Combretum bush; steekgras and Eragrostis grow thickly here, perhaps too thickly after the good summer rains. Patches of rooigras (Themeda triandra) a favourite of all the grazers, have been eaten right down. A Puffback shrike calls and a Red-billed hoopoe swoops into a knob-thorn tree.

Just west of us, on the eastern bank of the Sand river Harry Kirkman once had a nasty experience with a lion – he bears the scars to this day. After he retired from service in the Kruger Park, Harry had returned to Toulon as the Sabi Sand ranger. It was during this period, during the late 1950s that the son of the owner of Flockfield persuaded Harry to take him out to shoot a lion. Harry had been dining with the family, and they had heard lion around the camp. Harry and the young lad spotted a lion, which the boy missed with his first shot, and only wounded with his second. Harry felt it wiser not to try and follow the lion that night, but to wait until the following morning. He, the boy and a tracker went out just after sunrise, and spoored the lion, who appeared to have gone into the reeds on the bank of the river. Harry's tracker was convinced that had the lion still been in the reeds, they would have heard it. As they were turning to move up the bank, the lion sprang at Harry. He swung his rifle around, but its sling caught in the reeds and he was unable to shoot. The lion grabbed Harry's hand, at the same time pushing him over. Harry found himself on his back with the lion on top of him – his whiskers tickling Harry's face. Harry shouted 'Shoot him' to the lad, whose shot broke the lion's jaw, which meant Kirkman's hand was released. The lion again hid in the reeds, but they were able to follow him, and using one hand Harry was able to shoot the lion dead. The escapade meant a long stay in hospital for Kirkman.

At the Mamba waterhole, which in autumn was covered with the dainty yellow flowers of the water-lily (Nymphoides thunbergiana) and where warthogs wallow, there is now caked dry mud; the warthogs must go elsewhere for their mud baths, which are such a necessary part of their routine as the mud serves as a protection against biting insects as well as helping them to keep cool. South of the waterhole we approach an open area where the grass is short and the bush sparse. Beneath one

Male Puffback shrike

21

Wild dog.

of the few bushes, we notice the movement of large dark ears; two Wild dogs lie in the shade. Just beyond them eleven puppies romp lazily in the centre of the road. Behind and to the side of the cluster of youngsters are a further nine adult dogs, all relaxing in the sun, outstretched, just like domestic dogs. The puppies gnaw at each other's paws and tails playfully, and make puppy noises. The colouring of these animals is a strange mixture of black, white and yellow blotches; the tails are bushy and white; ears are great black saucers.

We slowly approach the two adults lying under the bush; they rise slowly and stretch their long rangy legs, looking at us fearlessly. They appear well fed. The ranger tells us that when the pups are young they are well-secreted, usually in a disused anthill hidden by bush. Wild dog (who are a definite species and not domestic dogs gone wild) work and live within a cohesive interdependent pack system. Hunting usually takes place during the daylight hours, the dogs relying on their sight, sense of smell, incredible speed and stamina. They are able to chase their prey at speeds of up to fifty kilometres an hour, a rate which they can maintain for several kilometres. The running is done by one or two dogs, the rest of the pack keeping behind at a steady, slower pace; when the leaders fall back, others take their place, until the prey is exhausted and overtaken by the dogs, who tear flesh from the animal while it is still alive. The prey is consumed at a tremendous rate. Babies and old and infirm dogs are the joint responsibility of the pack. Not only the mother, but other members of the pack regurgitate food for the babies. Old and infirm pack-members are treated in the same way and are well-looked after. I find this an endearing trait in these animals whose method of killing has resulted in their being generally regarded as loathsome.

We continue southwards for a while, and then cross the Sand river and begin our return journey up the western side of the river. The vegetation is different here. It is almost park-like, great Acacia nigrescens (knob-thorn trees) and marulas stand in the shortish tawny grass. Some of the marula trees have tiny reddish flowerlets and new leaves sprouting from the ends of their dry grey branches. The knob-

22

No two colour patterns of these fascinating hunters are identical.

thorns too are flowering here, where the comparative shelter is bringing them into flower earlier than those further north.

As we turn northwards along the Skukuza road, four Spotted hyena lope into sight. The animal in the lead has a large chunk of steenbuck in its jaws. Heads down, broad, round, dark-eared, their strong forequarters giving them a sloping appearance, they slink across the road in front of us and disappear into the bush. Perhaps the hyena in the vanguard is a mother taking food to her young. Spotted hyena have a matriarchal system, each clan ranging over a large territory, and although mostly scavengers do hunt smallish animals.

Wildebeest and zebra graze together some distance off the road. The wildebeest are the first to take fright at our approach, but turn to look at us from a safe distance. They have a slightly deferential, almost apologetic air, it seems to me. I love the dark black faces of the males, and the straggly beards – and their smooth rounded rumps. The zebra, a party consisting of a stallion, three mares and two youngsters, begin to trot off as we drive towards them, and then break into a canter, their short striped manes rippling as they move. They all look in superb condition, their beautiful pyjama-like coats fitting them to perfection. Each zebra has a unique pattern of black and beige (shadow) stripes. Our ranger explains that it is thought that the stripes may serve to confuse a predator during the chase, as well as camouflaging the animals as they graze in the dappled shade of the trees; we notice how effective is the latter, as the animals stop some distance away and lower their heads to feed.

Spotted hyena.

Wildebeest, turning to look at us from a safe distance.

Solitary Black-backed jackal, handsome in his winter garb, slinking off into the bush.

Further on we stop to watch a pair of African Hawk eagles sitting high in the branches of a dead tree. The female is larger than the male, as is the case, we are told, with most birds of prey. Weight-for-weight, these birds are the most powerful of the eagles, preying mostly on gamebirds.

In the distance, in a patch of shortish grass, a solitary Black-backed jackal stands for a moment, and then slinks off into the cover of the bush. At the airstrip a herd of impala ewes raise their heads to stare at us as we drive by. Baboons move through the bush to the left of us.

The sun is high in the north as we drive under the boom and back to camp.

Seedpods of the Large-fruited bushwillow ~ Combretum zeyheri.

Lucky Bean creeper ~ Abrus precatorius subs. africanus.

The seeds are extremely poisonous. I found this specimen twining through a small hole in a stump of a dead leadwood tree.

EARLY HISTORY

Sable antelope - a photograph taken at MalaMala in the 1920's

MalaMala is situated in the centre of the Transvaal lowveld, a low-lying region of flat bush country which stretches from the Crocodile river in the south to the Limpopo in the north, and between the great escarpment of the Drakensberg mountains on the west and the Lebombo mountains on the Moçambique border on the east. There is a magic about the South African lowveld which casts its spell on all who live there, and most who visit. In his foreword to Colonel Stevenson

Hamilton's book on the lowveld, Field Marshal Jan Smuts wrote '… in her heart … she is and remains free, unaffected by the invading influences … nowhere is that mysterious presence of Wild Africa felt more deeply than in the Transvaal lowveld…' and he added that greater even than the wonder of its scenery and flora and fauna is the 'mysterious eerie spirit which broods over this vast solitude…'.

The locality of the lowveld contributed largely to that spirit of freedom and solitude. Because of its latitude and elevation, malarial mosquitoes thrived in the hot wet summer months, and tsetse flies, which carried the dreaded nagana (sleeping sickness) infected humans and decimated domestic stock. So for centuries nature kept man and his civilization at bay, and the fauna, flora, trees and grasses were left in peace in this sanctuary.

Stone Age man lived here many thousands of years ago: evidence of his existence being artifacts, some of which have been found on the small hill Sithlawayise, which is on the eastern side of the Sand river at MalaMala.

Then came the Bushmen: little brown-skinned people, direct descendants of Stone Age man. They hunted antelope with bows and arrows fashioned from the trees, and gathered food from the veld around them. Nomadic, simple folk, their nature and way of life were in complete harmony with their environment. Perhaps it was this sensitivity which prompted members of the 'San' to ornament their cave dwellings with colourful paintings depicting their hunting activities. These paintings were executed with both skill and permanence, so that not only have many survived the ravages of time and weather, but they remain as accurate records of the species of animals which roamed the veld at that time. Examples of this rock art can be seen near Skukuza in the Kruger Park, about twenty kilometres south of MalaMala.

There is evidence that Arab traders traversed the lowveld centuries ago, en route from the east coast to the northern parts of the sub-continent, where they carried on an extensive trade in slaves, ivory and gold, which was mined in the legendary kingdom of Monomatapa. The east coast of Africa had been linked to the Mediterranean and Arab world since before Christ. In the Old Testament, in the Book of Kings, we read that Solomon sent an expedition to the southern 'far country' which brought back 'gold, silver, ivory and apes...'. Here was the source of the riches of the Queen of Sheba, some of which she took with her when she went to Jerusalem to visit the temple of King Solomon. In early maps of southern Africa, even as late as the mid-eighteenth century, the 'Empire of Monomatapa' is shown extending from the present day Zimbabwe to just south of the Tropic of Capricorn.

Black people had no doubt lived in tsetse-free parts of the lowveld since the first black migration from the north. In the eighteenth century, the first Portuguese explorers recorded meeting black people who were on the whole friendly. These scattered tribes lived in comparative peace until the early nineteenth century, when they came under the overpowering influence of what was called the 'Mfecane' – the

Black warriors dancing. 1838.
(C. Bell).   (Africana Museum)

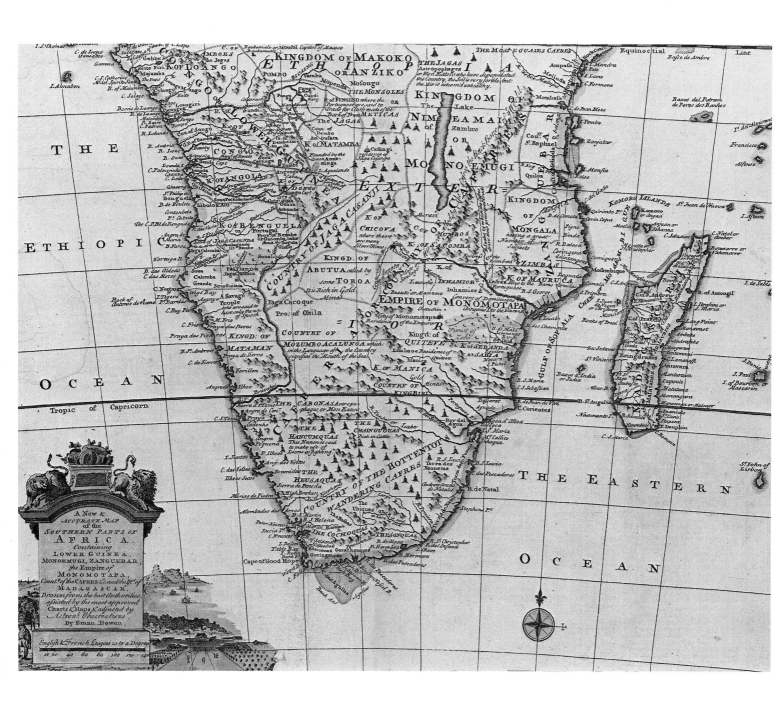

Map of southern Africa, drawn in 1747, showing the empire of Monomatapa.

'crushing'. In 1817 Shaka, who was to be called the Black Napoleon of Africa, succeeded Dingiswayo, and became the despotic 'king' of the Zulus. It was his aim to subjugate all the black tribes and bring them under his dominion. One of his generals, Soshangane, took his impi of about eight hundred men and went on the rampage to the north. His western flank invaded the lowveld, annihilating everything in its path, driving the Portuguese into the sea, and subduing the black tribes. These conquered tribes were given the name baThonga, and it is from these baThonga that the baTshangane or Shangaans developed. A great proportion of blacks in the lowveld today are Shangaans, whose language is closely allied to that spoken by the Zulus. Soshangane formed the Gaza empire where he held dominion from just north of Delagoa Bay up the coast as far as the Zambesi river.

The Dutch, since their colonization of the Cape in 1652, had always been intrigued by stories of the golden riches of Monomatapa; in fact Jan van Riebeeck mounted an expedition in 1660 to find Monomatapa. This and two subsequent expeditions failed to reach their destination. In 1719 the Council of Seventeen in Holland ordered the political council at the Cape to take possession of Delagoa Bay, which would provide them not only with access to the hinterland, but with a port for the export of the riches which they believed they would find. The Dutch East India Company held Delagoa Bay from 1721 to 1732. During their occupation the Dutch mounted an expedition of thirty-one men under the leadership of a man called De Cuiper. Not only was he intrepid, he was also literate. In the journal which De Cuiper kept we read that on June 10 1725, two weeks after leaving the coast, he and his men crossed what is now called the Crocodile river and headed northwards, thus being the first white men to set foot on land which would one day become the Kruger National Park. De Cuiper and his party travelled as far as the drift across the Sabi river, near the present Skukuza camp, before an encounter with hostile blacks forced him to retreat eastwards to the safety of the Lebombo mountains. Two years later De Cuiper died of the fever which he had contracted during his abortive adventure.

One hundred years were to pass before another white man would pass this way and chronicle his adventures.

Captain Cornwallis Harris, an officer in the East India Company's Corps of Engineers, spent two years of his sick leave (from 1836-1838) hunting and exploring the hinterland of Southern Africa from the Cape to the Limpopo. Fortunately Harris was not only a hunter; he recorded with pen and brush his adventures in the exciting and sparsely populated regions of the sub-continent. He recounted meetings with black tribesmen, with parties of the first Boer trekkers which he met as they made their intrepid way from the Cape and British domination; and in delicate and fairly accurate water-colour he painted the animals which he observed. To this English naturalist and huntsman goes the honour of being the first white man to observe an 'unusually dark antelope' which he realized was new to science. He described the 'magnificent coal-black bucks… with scimitar-shaped horns'… and stated that he wanted one of these 'rather than all the elephants of Africa'. This was the first recorded sighting of the beautiful animal whose head is the emblem, and after which MalaMala is named – the Sable antelope – Hippotragus niger – once called the 'Harrisbuck'. Harris shot a large male, painted its likeness and sent his specimen to the British Museum. Although the area where Harris first saw these Sable is not clearly described, he stated that it was to the east of the 'Matabili' country, so we can assume that he may well have travelled in that part of the lowveld where the animals flourished.

Between 1836 and 1837 two parties of trekkers, each with nine wagons, crossed the Vaal river and made their way northwards, not only to seek pastures new far removed from the authority of the British, but also to establish a link with a sea-port on the east coast. Once in the northern Transvaal the trekker leaders parted company, Van Rensburg taking his party to the north east, hoping to find a gap through the Lebombo range. Louis Trichardt, the other leader, elected to wait at the foot of the Zoutpansberg mountains until word should come from Van Rensburg

30

Major Sir William Cornwallis Harris. c. 1844.
(Africana Museum)

Sable Antelope –
painted by Cornwallis Harris.
He was the first person to
record this animal.

An etching by W. H. Coetzer of an event which occurred
during Louis Trichardt's trek into the eastern Transvaal.
(Africana Museum)

that the latter had been successful. Van Rensburg and his entire party were annihilated by Soshangane's men on the south bank of the Limpopo river, probably where Pafuri is today. Trichardt, having waited in vain for news, set his course south-eastwards in an endeavour to find his own route to the Portuguese coast. His party encountered no hostility from tribesmen, but nagana and fever took their toll of both man and beast. And there were other hazards. Trichardt wrote in his diary that as they trekked beside the Sand river their cattle fell prey to both lion and to the ticks which lurked in the long grass. The present road from Newington to MalaMala is thought to have been part of the route the trekkers used. Trichardt eventually reached the coast in 1838. Only twenty-six souls survived the difficult journey; they later sailed from Delagoa Bay to Port Natal.

The first white man to settle in the lowveld was of Portuguese extraction. In 1840 Joao Albasini, a lad of nineteen, was instructed by his father, an Italian sea-captain, to establish a safari trading route into the interior from Delagoa Bay. This Albasini junior did with enthusiasm. Not only did he organize regular safaris but he established a half-way trading post where goods could be transferred from black porters to ox-wagons which carried the goods to destinations on the highveld. Joao

Jowawa Albasini's flamboyant signature on a document of 1855
(Africana Museum)

(called Jowawa by the natives) settled on the banks of the Sabi river, near the present Pretorius Kop camp in the Kruger Park, and built himself a modest stone dwelling, the remains of which can still be seen. Jowawa kept cattle which he had bartered from one of the local black chiefs, grew grain, hunted venison for himself and his porters, and organized elephant hunts for ivory which was sent to the coast to his father's ships. The trade soon developed into a flourishing business. Albasini was always on good terms with his black neighbours, and became the uncrowned 'king' of the lowveld. His idyllic existence ended when in 1847 he married the niece of one of the trekkers and his wife persuaded him to leave his riverside paradise and move to the comparative civilization of the newly-founded town of Ohrigstad in the Lydenburg district. In the southern area of the Kruger Park large Portuguese crosses have been found carved into the bark of some old leadwood trees. Some think this to have been the work of Jowawa – perhaps marking the boundaries of his little lowveld kingdom.

With the arrival of more trekkers into the Transvaal and the establishment of the Ohrigstad Republic, Boers began drifting into the regions of high land to the west and south-west of the lowveld. In the winter months, when danger of fever had passed, these new settlers would trek down to the lowveld with their wagons to hunt. There was little money in circulation among these people, and game was regarded as a means of livelihood, hides being a commodity which could be bartered for life's necessities. By 1846 game in the lowveld had become so reduced that the Volksraad of the Ohrigstad Republic passed a resolution which stated that 'wanton' destruction of game was prohibited, and that only game that was 'reasonably' needed could be shot. Twelve years later the Transvaal Republic's first game law was passed, which stipulated that only game required for a person's own consumption could be hunted, or that which could be loaded on to one wagon (which is itself an indication of the extent of the slaughter which took place in the winter months). Furthermore, no game could be killed solely for hides. These proclamations were not able to be enforced,

33

Throughout South Africa, the slaughter of game was the order of the day.

(Africana Museum)

however. The Boer was by nature a law unto himself and had always regarded game as something to be shot. He continued to use his annual winter trek into the lowveld as an opportunity to fill his wagons with skins and biltong (dried meat). So although no one at this time lived permanently in the area of MalaMala, in the winter months the veld would resound to the noise of the hunters' guns, while at night plumes of smoke rose from the fires around the wagons. Great logs of the leadwood tree would be felled, which because of the hard nature of the wood, would burn continuously for the duration of the hunters' visit.

By the 1860s trouble between white elephant hunters and black tribesmen in the northern Transvaal (in what is now the independent homeland of Venda) had been brewing for some time. Although a law had been passed to prohibit this, the white men had been supplying the blacks with powerful elephant guns. These guns were now being used against their former owners. A young man, one of South Africa's famous sons, whose name in later years would be indelibly linked with game conservation, was detailed to raise a commando to quell this uprising in the north. The young Paul Kruger had difficulty in persuading men to join his commando. The Boer settlers were reluctant to leave their new farms, and by 1868 Kruger had been able to muster only two hundred and sixty men, most of whom were 'foreigners' – diggers who had trekked to the Transvaal in search of gold. With this small band of men, Kruger fought a losing battle at Makapaan's Poort. One of the members of Kruger's commando may well have been a Scot called John McNab, who the following year became the first owner of the farm MalaMala.

In 1869 the name MalaMala (which is the Shangaan word for the Sable antelope) appears for the first time, written in copperplate on a parchment-like official document. This Deed of Grant bestowed the quitrent farm MalaMala on John McNab for the sum of £1.10s which had to be paid annually. In that year several quitrent farms were granted as 'Burger right farms', where the farm was granted for some service which had been rendered, and although annual 'rent' had to be paid, the

The young Paul Kruger. Believed to be the only existing photograph showing his mutilated thumb. (From: The Memoirs of Paul Kruger, Vol. 1. 1902)

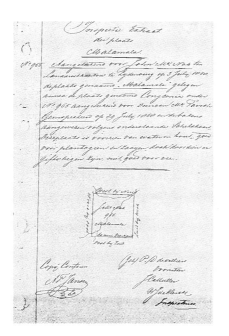
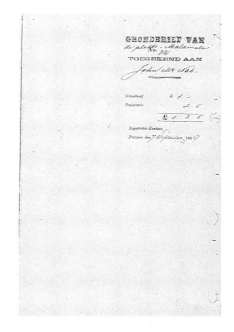
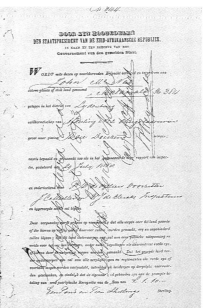

Facsimile of the first title deed of the farm Malamala. Signed by Marthinus Wessels Pretorius, president of the Transvaal Republic.

owner was granted full title to the land. We can assume that in McNab's case the grant may well have been for serving in Kruger's commando. The recipient, apart from paying the sum of money annually, had also to make himself available for further call-up at any time, in which case he had to provide a horse, saddle, rifle and ammunition, and three days' rations for himself. This title deed, which was signed by Marthinus Wessels Pretorius, the President of the Transvaal Republic, stipulated that the owner of MalaMala was to grant people the right to 'outspan' on the farm, to allow grazing for travellers, and to preserve any existing roads or tracks on the farm. From this it can be assumed that MalaMala was in those days an area traversed by travellers; a likely supposition, as the Sand river flowed perenially through the farm from north to south. Included in the documents of sale is a sketch of the farm, together with a statement that water and wood were plentiful, but that the farm was not suitable for cattle.

We do not know anything about McNab, or whether he lived on his farm or used it for winter grazing, but twenty-four years later, in 1893, in the District Court of Lydenburg, the matter of *The State v McNab, J.* was heard, following which a court order deprived McNab of his farm on the grounds of non-payment. Further, goods were removed to cover a debt of £84.5s.

John Wylie Craig Niven bought the farm outright in 1893, by an order of the court, for £185. On Niven's instructions MalaMala was surveyed for the first time, by the Government surveyor WH Gilfillan.

In 1872 alluvial gold was found in the Lydenburg area of the Transvaal, which precipitated a gold-rush to the Transvaal escarpment. Diggers came in large numbers from the diamond diggings at Kimberley, where large mining companies were ousting the small-time miner.

As the gold diggings flourished and grew, a regular trade route to the coast at Delagoa Bay was needed to transport goods and machinery. Black porters, who proved more resistant to malaria, were still being used, but ox-wagons were becoming necessary to carry the increasingly heavy supplies. Where tsetse fly infestations were concentrated, a dash

Gold-digging at Pilgrims' Rest, Lydenburg area circa 1875
(Africana Museum)

THE CREEK PILGRIMS REST

was made at night by the wagons, in order to avoid the cattle being infected by the insects. But losses were still heavy, the journey was arduous and dangerous, and sometimes took months to complete.

In 1875 a young Hungarian-born adventurer, Alois Hugo Nellmapius, who was later to become one of the first entrepreneurs and great landowners of the Transvaal, persuaded the Volksraad to give him the right to build a road from the diggings to the Transvaal-Portuguese border at Komatipoort, more or less following Albasini's old wagon road. The Volksraad welcomed the scheme, and granted Nellmapius the concession, which included farms, each of 3 000 morgen, situated fifteen miles (twenty-four kilometres) apart along the proposed road. On these farms Nellmapius established resting stations and storage depots, each supervised by a manager. Nellmapius was granted a similar concession by the Portuguese authorities. Thus the Lourenço-Marques and South African Republic Transport Company was formed. Using black porters and donkeys instead of oxen to draw the wagons, Nellmapius, in February 1876, began transporting goods along the road he hacked from the bush. The Nellmapius road operated successfully until another black uprising – this time concerning the chief of the baPedi, Sekukuni – brought the gold-diggings to a standstill. Some of the miners joined the commando raised to deal with the matter; black workers either joined Sekukuni or fled to their homes. When the dust had settled, Nellmapius had lost most of his porters, several of his store managers had been murdered, others had deserted. His transport company was in ruins. He was, however, still in possession of his farms, owning large tracts of land between the Crocodile and Sand rivers.

(As so often occurred in the history of South Africa, it was men such as Nellmapius – young, solitary, frequently 'foreign' – who took the initiative, blazed trails, and became significant contributors to the economic development of their adopted land. Later, when Nellmapius left the Lydenburg goldfields, he bought land near Pretoria and began farming on a scale and in a scientific manner unknown in the country at that time. He called his farm 'Irene' after his daughter; part of his land, Doornkop, became the home of Field Marshal Jannie Smuts. A Swiss veterinarian whom Nellmapius imported to care for his livestock – Dr Arnold Theiler – later founded South Africa's world famous veterinary research institute Onderstepoort).

At the conclusion of the Sekukuni 'war', the coffers of the Transvaal Republic were somewhat empty, and it was apparent that the Government was having difficulty in controlling the black tribes. In April 1877 the British annexed the Transvaal in order to restore law and order to the country north of the Vaal river. This annexation lasted only until 1880 when the Boers rose to fight the so-called First Boer War, and

Alois Hugo Nellmapius: adventurer, man of property; founder of the Lourenço-Marques – South African Republic Transport Company. Here he is dressed up in his uniform as Portuguese Consul to the S.A. Republic. (Africana Museum)

with the final battle when the British were defeated at Majuba Hill in 1881, regained their independence.

Mining in the Lydenburg-Pilgrim's Rest area was taken over by syndicates and companies, the most notable being the Transvaal Gold Exploration and Land Company. A new gold-rush which drove the diggers to areas further east, began in 1884, when the Barber brothers discovered a gold-bearing reef at the foot of the Drakensberg mountains (less than 100 kilometres south of MalaMala). The site was named Barberton, which soon proliferated into a bustling mining town, where the country's first stock exchange was started. At Barberton another of South Africa's famous personalities made his appearance, first as a storeman, and later running with transport wagons along the Nellmapius road to Delagoa Bay. Because of this man's account of his travels through the bushveld with his dog, the name of the road was eventually changed to 'Jock of the Bushveld Road' and Jock, Sir Percy Fitzpatrick's dog, became immortalized. The bushveld, with all its

Sir Percy Fitzpatrick, the author of Jock of the Bushveld.
(Africana Museum)

South Africa's first Stock Exchange. Barberton 1886-1889
(Africana Museum)

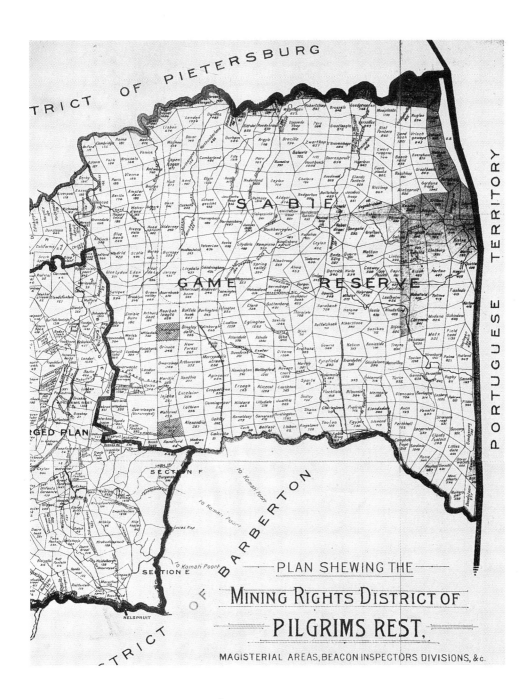

PLAN SHEWING THE

MINING RIGHTS DISTRICT OF

PILGRIMS REST,

MAGISTERIAL AREAS, BEACON INSPECTORS DIVISIONS, &c.

The Sabi Game Reserve. Proclaimed in 1898. Malamala is
listed as farm Nº 384, situated in the centre of the reserve.

hunting charm and spirit, was put memorably and unforgettably on to paper.

Three years later, with yet another discovery of gold, there was a change of interest and a rush of unprecedented proportions to the latest Eldorado – the Transvaal Witwatersrand. The Eastern Transvaal slipped back into more or less peaceful obscurity.

But things were not quite as before.

In 1884, a year after he had been elected President of the Transvaal Republic, Paul Kruger, always a man of the veld, had suggested that a sanctuary should be established to protect what was left of the game in the Transvaal. His plea had fallen on deaf ears. Now, twelve years later, with the Volksraad's coffers swelled by the rich new gold discoveries, the completion of a railway-line linking Pretoria with Delagoa Bay, and the miraculous disappearance of the tsetse fly from the Transvaal as the result of the rinderpest epidemic in 1896, Kruger's pipe-dream could become a reality.

In March 1898 the Sabie Game Reserve was proclaimed, consisting of the low areas lying between the Crocodile and Sabi rivers, in extent 4 660 square kilometres (1 000 square miles). Penalties were prescribed for the protection of game, but as the only control was exercised by the police sergeant at Komatipoort, hunting continued as before. The destruction of the game increased with the construction of the Selati Line, a railway linking the goldfields in the east with the Pretoria-Delagoa Bay line at Komatipoort. This rail link had been proposed by Kruger in 1890, and commenced three years later. With the exposure of bribery and corruption indulged in by the Belgian construction company and practically all the members of the Volksraad (on a scale unprecedented in this Calvinistic corner of the world), the line was abandoned after only 100 kilometres had been laid. Tools and equipment were downed; the workers simply walked away. In 1909 when construction was recommenced, some of the equipment was still where it had been left sixteen years previously. Visitors to MalaMala can see the stone ballast of a section of this line which runs to the north-west across the southern

42

Construction of the
Delagoa Bay railway
line - 1898.
(Africana Museum)

part of the present Sabi Sand Wildtuin. It was decided to remove this part of the line in the 1950s, because of the hazard which it presented to the game.

Tales about the old Selati Line abound. It is said that during the original construction, fever took its toll to the extent that a man died for each sleeper laid. A little blue-painted cross marks the grave of one of these workers (it can be seen on the left-hand side of the road from Skukuza Airport to MalaMala); but this man, CC Maloney died 1894 not from malaria, but at the hands of his workers, who, having slain him, buried him on the spot. There were no official stations on this section of the line, only sidings and plate-layers' cottages. One white man, with fifteen black gangers, was responsible for each fifteen miles (twenty-four kilometres) of track. Transport for the workers was by means of a pump trolley on which the white man and his tools reposed, while his gangers pushed. The ganger's job was to keep the line clear for the once-a-week passage of the train. Wild animals were a real nuisance, as were saplings which grew on the track in the rainy season. In his

43

Steamer on the old
Selati line c 1895
Africana Museum)

book *South African Eden* Colonel Stevenson-Hamilton recalls meeting
the train when, in 1904 he was on his way to the Sabie Game Reserve for
the first time: '...puffing along at a reckless fifteen miles an hour'. This
train was to play a vital role in the lives of the landowners of the area,
when in the 1920s they paid winter visits to their game farms.

During the Boer War (1899-1902) there was some activity on the
Selati line. The Boers used the Pretoria-Delagoa line to transport arms
and supplies which they had imported through Lourenço Marques. The
line therefore became one of the targets of the British forces. Lord
Kitchener built several blockhouses along it in an effort to contain
guerilla activity of the wily Boers. The nearest blockhouse to MalaMala
was built at Komatipoort. However activity came closer when a wild
character of dubious origin called 'Major' Steinacker made his

44

appearance. This soldier of fortune, with a band of conscripts, known locally as the 'Forty Thieves', but officially as 'Steinacker's Horse', based himself at Komatipoort and proceeded to represent British military interests there. About the only undertaking of any consequence which Steinacker's Horse achieved was an attempt to prevent the Boers from reaching Komatipoort. Steinacker and his men blew up a culvert on the Crocodile river side of the town, but unfortunately the Boers had already passed that way, and Steinacker's action served only to halt the arrival of the British. During the twenty-four hours which it took them to repair the culvert, the Boers had escaped northwards up the Selati line. Steinacker built a blockhouse guarding the drift of the Sabi river, which later became Stevenson Hamilton's first home when he became the Sabie Reserve's first warden. Apart from these two 'contributions'

"Major" Steinacker of Steinacker's Horse. 1899-1902
(Africana Museum)

Steinacker and his forty thieves did little else than help to decrease even further the game population of the area. He and his men were as partial to hunting and the consumption of venison as they were to drinking vast quantities of whisky which they believed was a prophylactic against malaria.

Yet despite the decimation of the game in the area, Denys Reitz, in his book *Commando*, which is an account of his service in the Second Boer War, describes travelling through the 'Sabi low country' and seeing '…great herds of zebra, wildebeest and sable… and at night lions'. He described the country as being '…as untouched as that upon which the old pioneers had looked when they first came north in the days of the Great Trek'. Later, as the young Reitz waited at the border town of Komatipoort before leaving his defeated land at the end of the war in 1902, his father gave him this short verse to take with him into his self-imposed exile:

> South Africa
> Whatever foreign shores my feet must tread
> My hopes for thee are not yet dead
> Thy freedom's sun may for a while be set
> But not forever. God does not forget.

A few years later, Reitz was persuaded by the wife of Jannie Smuts to return from Madagascar. He became Minister of Lands in 1919 in Smuts' Government, and was instrumental in the passing of a law which would protect the bushveld which he so dearly loved.

And so the devastating Boer War ended, and South Africa began a new era in which game preservation was to become if not a priority, a reality. The winter hunting of the Trek Boers, hunting by Boer commandos and men of Steinacker's Horse, the shooting of game by the construction workers on the Selati Line, had all taken their toll. When the new warden arrived to take up his position of the newly-proclaimed Sabie Game Reserve in 1902, he was struck by the paucity of the game in the south. He was also faced with the daunting task of establishing some sort of control over a vast tract of land consisting of government-owned land interspersed with privately-owned farms. The land in the lowveld had been undergoing changes of ownership.

In 1890 Nellmapius, who had found himself in financial difficulties, transferred ownership of his lowveld farms to the firm of Werner, Beit & Co (the forerunners of the Corner House organization). With the two million acres they thus acquired (not for 2 shillings an acre as first suggested, but in exchange for paying Nellmapius' debt of £10 000 to Lewis & Marks), Werner, Beit & Co had control of four million acres of land in the Transvaal. They floated a company of 100 000 shares which they registered as the Transvaal Consolidated Land and Exploration Company, known as the TCL, a company which is still in existence. There were other large property developers which owned land in the lowveld; old maps show the names of the Transvaal Estate and Development Co, Henderson Transvaal Estates, Oceana Company, Transvaal Exploration Lands and Mines, and others. In 1902 Stevenson Hamilton journeyed to Pretoria and Johannesburg and visited all the landowners personally. The landowners all agreed that in return for services which the staff of the Reserve would render, the various companies would transfer control of their farms to the Government for a period of five years. The boundaries of the Reserve were extended twelve miles to the west, and by 1904 included the area between the Crocodile and Olifants rivers to north and south, and from the Lebombo mountains on the east to $31^{1}/_{2}°$ west. MalaMala was now within the Sabie Game Reserve.

Between 1905 and 1914 Stevenson Hamilton, backed by a small group of supporters, waged a continuing struggle against the farmers in the Lydenburg district. Traditionally these farmers had used the lowveld for winter grazing for their sheep. In fact the move to the lowveld in the winter months had involved a wholesale trek which included not only the livestock but the entire family, who enjoyed what was their annual

Colonel James Stevenson-Hamilton, Chief warden of the Sabie Game Reserve, which later developed into the Kruger National Park.

(Africana Museum)

Transvaal farmers camping beside their wagons during their annual winter trek to the lowveld.

(Africana Museum)

holiday in the bush, camping beside the wagons, watching the grazing herds and hunting both for the pot and for a summer's supply of biltong.

Now that source of winter grass was situated within the precincts of the Reserve. Matters came to a head when the farmers threatened to withdraw their farms from the Reserve unless the grazing continued. This would have so fragmented the Reserve that it would have been doomed. Stevenson Hamilton decided to permit grazing on the farms from May through September under certain conditions: no hunting was permitted and a charge of £5 per area was levied to cover the cost of policing the area.

This arrangement proved unsatisfactory to all parties: the levy proved insufficient to pay the cost of using rangers to patrol the areas, and the farmers complained that lion were eating their stock, and that they

The old Boer-war blockhouse, built at the drift across the Sabi river, where Skukuza camp is today. This was Colonel Stevenson-Hamilton's first home.
(Africana Museum)

should be permitted to shoot any carnivores. By 1914 the future of the Reserve looked bleak indeed. Stevenson Hamilton returned from the war to find his game sadly reduced by poaching as well as from the increased numbers of carnivores. Rumblings concerning the ban on hunting became a roar.

There were other developments concerning the big landowning companies which were to add to Stevenson-Hamilton's problems.

It was not until after the Great War that any move was made in South Africa to encourage agricultural and ranching activities. Up to that time, food for the growing towns and cities had been largely imported. Now efforts were made to encourage local production. There was a great need to increase the country's cattle herds which had been almost totally decimated by the rinderpest epidemic of 1896 and then by the two Boer Wars. (By 1904 there were only an estimated three and a half million head of cattle in South Africa). As farming activities increased, so land values rose, and it was to the sparsely-populated northern and eastern parts of the Transvaal that farmers were looking to satisfy their need for land.

In 1896 John Niven had sold MalaMala to Louis Joel of Johannesburg, in a parcel of four farms, for £1 075. During the following twenty years ownership changed seven times, each transaction involving Johannesburg-based owners. It was at the beginning of 1921 that the farm was acquired by the Transvaal Consolidated Land and Investment Company, when Sir Pieter de Villiers-Graaff (father of Sir de Villiers-Graaff, a wellknown South African political figure) sold the farm for £1 820 2s 6d Graaff had purchased MalaMala himself a month previously in order to help a friend who was in financial trouble. The TCL had now consolidated its lowveld land holdings even further.

In a sales brochure produced by the TCL in 1922 MalaMala appears as one of their many farms for sale. MalaMala was described as being 'Very excellent for cattle. Good water. Suitable for maize, groundnuts. Rainfall 25 inches. 6 miles to rail'. Terms of sale were attractive; one fifth of the purchase price down, the balance payable over ten years at 5

50

percent. Prices of the company's farms ranged from 5 shillings to 30 shillings an acre.

Because this land had never been farmed before, the TCL saw the advisability of stocking large tracts of their holdings with cattle, to demonstrate the viability of the land as ranching country. Stevenson-Hamilton believed that there were other and more sinister reasons behind the cattle ranching. He believed that the TCL, who by now had bought out most of the other landowners in the Reserve, were aiming at asserting their rights as farmers in the area, and that by establishing a cattle ranch in the middle of the Reserve as 'close as possible to the

Hunting party on the farm Toulon 1924.
(Photograph lent by Jenny Jooste)

warden's headquarters' (as he described it), they would try and force his (the warden's) hand by making things so impossible that he would put pressure on the Government to buy the Company's land. Stevenson-Hamilton wrote that not only did the TCL over-estimate his influence with the Government, but they also under-estimated Stevenson Hamilton himself. He was ready for any move the Company might make.

In 1922, 800 hundred head of cattle were transported by rail to the farm 'Toulon' (now part of Rattray Reserves, on which Kirkman's

T.C.L. cattle stockade on the farm Shaws, adjoining Toulon.
(Photograph lent by Jenny Jooste)

Camp is situated). A house was built for the manager, Crosby, who soon became a friend of Stevenson-Hamilton, in fact the warden rode to Toulon each week for Sunday lunch. In 1923 Crosby was instructed by the TCL to put the Reserve's protection laws to the test, and shot a wild animal. Crosby told the warden of the Company's plan. The latter advised Crosby to go ahead. Crosby then shot an animal – chosing an old wildebeest bull. The company was taken to court. Their defence was that the wildebeest had been found eating grass, and was therefore destroying the Company's crops. The case hinged on whether veld grass constituted a 'crop'. The magistrate in the Lydenburg Court held that it was not, a decision upheld by a higher court, to which the TCL took the matter. The case had dragged on for months, which was to the benefit of the Reserve, as it focused attention on the absurdity of cattle ranching in the middle of a game sanctuary. The publicity which the case engendered served to force the government to face the problem, and with the aid and enthusiastic support of men such as Denys Reitz, the Minister of Lands, it was decided not to buy the TCL farms but to withdraw the western boundary of the Reserve eastwards by fifteen miles. This removed one million acres of private land and 500 000 acres of government land, the latter being used to exchange with farmers who possessed land north of the present Reserve. The entire area from Punda Milia in the north to the Crocodile river in the south was consolidated. In 1926 a National Parks Act was passed, and the Kruger National Park proclaimed. As Stevenson-Hamilton wrote with justified pride: his Cinderella had at last become a princess.

On the western boundary of the new Park, MalaMala, together with the other farms belonging to the TCL was now independent of Reserve restrictions, and was about to enter a new era, as exciting and auspicious as that of its bushveld neighbour.

"If Winter comes can Spring be far behind?"
<u>Ode to the west wind.</u>   Shelley

Some   Malamala   "behinds".

54

Catopsilia florella ♀
African Migrant.

SPRING

'… And every winter change to spring.'
Tennyson, *In Memoriam*

Spring at MalaMala is a movable feast, depending for its advent on the arrival of the summer rains. In some of the larger trees however whose roots reach deep into the moisture well below the surface soil, the sap rises in response to a seasonal rhythm; green leaves sprout and buds begin to swell.

   The harbinger of spring in the bushveld is the Wild pear (Dombeya rotundifolia), whose delicate pale blossoms are eagerly awaited by bees, butterflies and sunbirds. There is also insect activity among the cream catkin-flowers of the knob-thorn trees (Acacia nigrescens). Tiny reddish buds sprout from the smooth grey stems of the marula trees, and the

Dombeya rotundifolia · Wild Pear.
Called by the Swazi's:
"umBikanyaka"~
"the herald of
the season".

Flowers of male
Marula tree —
Sclerocarya birrea.

View of the camp - Malamala.

56

At the foot of Sithlawayise: memorial plaques to Wac Campbell, Alec Logan, Dymock Crofts and Fred Macbeth.

New leaves of Transvaal ebony tree.

new leaves of young Transvaal ebony trees shine red in the thick bush near the river.

Not only are the buds on the trees swollen with the rising thrust of new life; so are many antelope. Zebra mares are heavily pregnant, as are the ubiquitous impala ewes. The latter begin dropping their young at the beginning of November, going off into the bush on their own to give birth. Usually all the impala babies have appeared before the end of the month. This type of seasonal breeding ensures that the young, born at the start of the wet season, will benefit from the maximum food supply in mid-summer. Their synchronized lambing (known as the Darling effect), results in a glut of babies. As impala lambs are particularly helpless just after birth, the flooding of the baby-market ensures that sufficient will survive the predators. Wildebeest also employ this tactic. We observe a herd of the latter on Eyrefield; in the centre of the dozen or so adults stands a solitary, pale, new-born calf. Born too early, the calf will doubtless fall prey to some predator. As Rudyard Kipling wrote:

Now this is the Law of the Jungle –
as old and as true as the sky;
And the wolf that shall keep it may
prosper, but the wolf that shall break
it must die.

Red-chested cuckoo

Black cuckoo

The warm weather is a signal for the return of those birds who have wintered in northern climes. The cuckoos are among the first migrants to return. As this is the start of their breeding season, the males call long and repetitively. The persistent call of the Piet-my-vrou (Red-chested cuckoo) rings out from every corner of the bush (and can be heard sometimes well into the night at camp); the Black cuckoo announces his return in his mournful voice – his call is amusingly but aptly interpreted as 'I'm *so*....sick', Jacobin Cuckoos flit in pairs in the trees at the

58

Jacobin cuckoo

Diederik cuckoo

Pardopsis punctatissima -
Polka Dot.

Masked weaver
nest.

Matshaphiri dam, and at the camp the Diederik cuckoo adds his
repetitious voice to that of the orioles and the loeries. Soon the cuckoos
will begin their egg-laying, depositing their eggs in the nests of other
birds, who will unwittingly hatch and rear the small imposters.

Spring is a time of general nest-building. The Masked and Spotted-
backed weavers, the males in bright yellow breeding plumage, strip
long strands from the reeds and weave their oval nests in a frenzy of
fanning wings and swizzling chatter. Dozens of nests hang from the
giant marula trees (Sclerocarya) in the camp. Beneath the trees, half-
woven nests, roughly torn from their moorings, lie discarded by the
fussy females. The eggs which the females will lay hatch when the green
seeds have formed on the grasses; the soft flowerheads of some grasses
are used now by the birds to line their skilfully-woven nests. At the
moment the busy males rush back and forth with building material in
their beaks; they must be grateful for the abundance of crumbs put out
for them each day in front of the diningroom, where they and the
Glossy starlings make such a gay picture of blue and yellow.

A Green pigeon, one of the most beautiful of the bush birds, sits
hatching her eggs in a nest of twigs built only
two metres from the ground in a young tree
at the camp. For about ten days she will sit
alone patiently waiting for the chicks to
emerge from the two white eggs.

The dawn chorus in springtime, which
starts as sky begins to lighten soon after
4 am, is a symphony of the calls of cuckoos,
bulbuls, hoopoes, barbets (both Crested and
Black-collared), Black-headed orioles, a
Kurrichane thrush, the clear bell-like tones of the
Orange-breasted shrike, and the raucous 'Kwaali-
kwaali' of the Natal francolin.
It is worth waking early to hear.

At six, while we sip our early-
morning coffee on the veranda, the

59

Jakkalsbessie fruit.

Eggs of
Kurrichane thrush

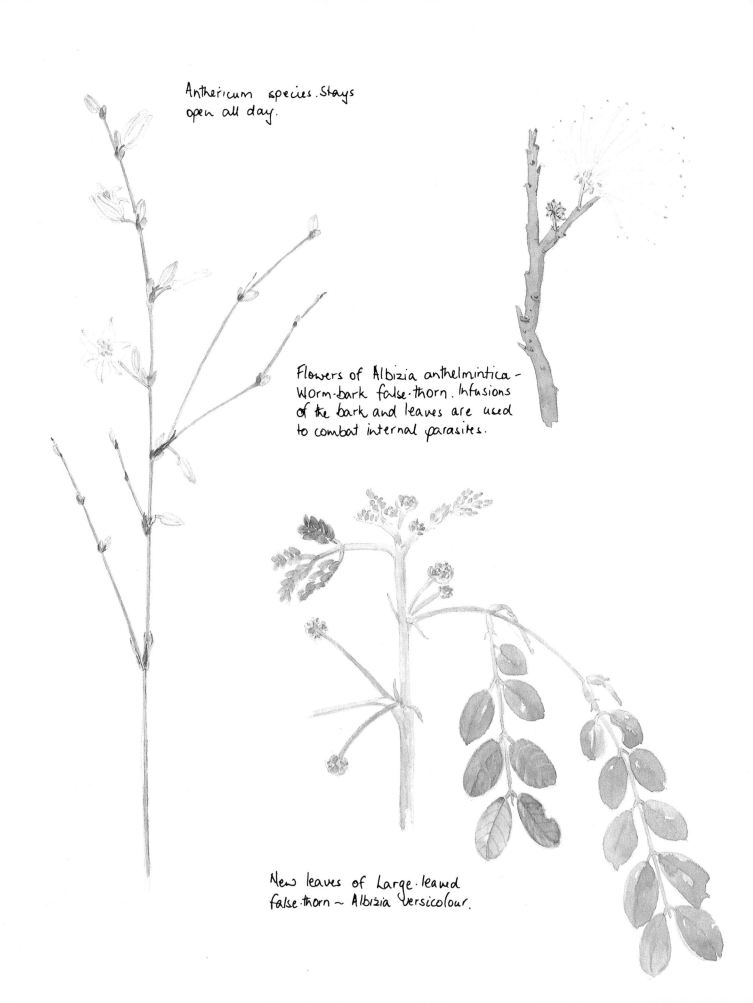

Anthericum species. Stays
open all day.

Flowers of Albizia anthelmintica –
Worm-bark false-thorn. Infusions
of the bark and leaves are used
to combat internal parasites.

New leaves of Large-leaved
false-thorn ~ Albizia Versicolour.

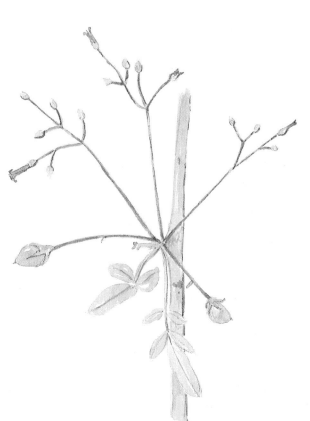

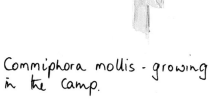

Commiphora mollis - growing
in the camp.

Spring growth of
Red Bushwillow, growing
near the old Selati line.

Gardenia volkensii - Transvaal gardenia.

Seeds of Flame creeper-
Combretum microphyllum.

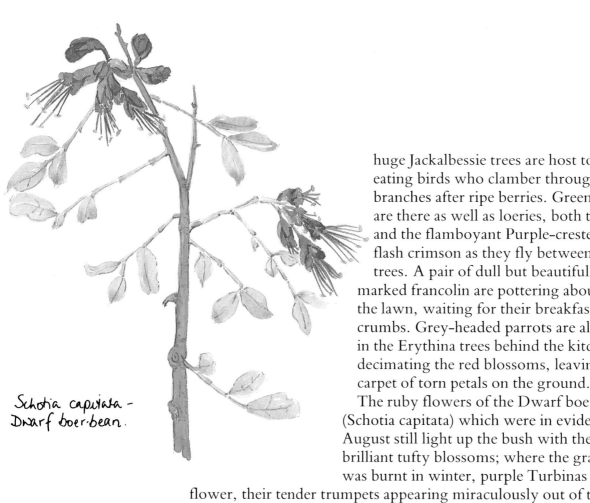

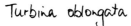
Schotia capitata –
Dwarf boer-bean.

huge Jackalbessie trees are host to fruit-eating birds who clamber through the branches after ripe berries. Green pigeons are there as well as loeries, both the Grey and the flamboyant Purple-crested, who flash crimson as they fly between the trees. A pair of dull but beautifully marked francolin are pottering about on the lawn, waiting for their breakfast crumbs. Grey-headed parrots are already in the Erythina trees behind the kitchens, decimating the red blossoms, leaving a carpet of torn petals on the ground.

The ruby flowers of the Dwarf boer-bean (Schotia capitata) which were in evidence in August still light up the bush with their brilliant tufty blossoms; where the grass was burnt in winter, purple Turbinas flower, their tender trumpets appearing miraculously out of the hard brown earth. In the stonier areas of Marthly, clumps of Handkerchief plant (Cycnium adonese) adorn the short green grass. These beautiful white flowers, whose other common name is Ink plant, are parasitic on the grass. The flowers become mottled with navy blue as if ink has been spilled on the petals; as the flowers fade they turn completely ink-blue. The zebrawood (Dalbergia melanoxylon) is flowering in profusion, honey-scented clusters hang from the thorny grey stems. Little golden balls are bursting on the Acacia tortilis trees, and on the river road the trailing stems of the Devil's thorn (Dicerocaryum zanguebarium) bear their lovely pink trumpets, soon to turn into the strange seeds equipped with a pair of vicious spikes, nasty for man and beast to tred upon.

Festooned over the bushes near the Sand river is the Combretum microphyllum – aptly named the Flame creeper. Already some of the pale pink and green pods have formed and hang between the tufty red flowers. Sweet-smelling sprays or bright yellow blossoms of the

Turbina oblongata

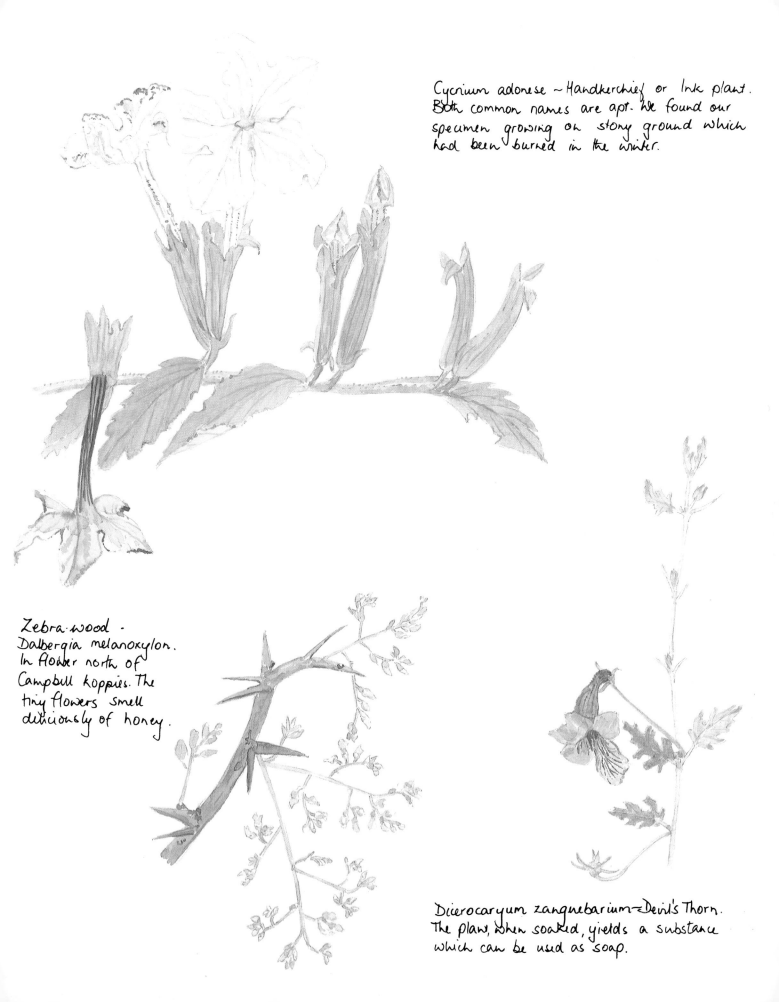

Cycnium adonense ~ Handkerchief or Ink plant.
Both common names are apt. We found our
specimen growing on stony ground which
had been burned in the winter.

Zebra-wood -
Dalbergia melanoxylon.
In flower north of
Campbell koppies. The
tiny flowers smell
deliciously of honey.

Dicerocaryum zanguebarium ~ Devil's Thorn.
The plant, when soaked, yields a substance
which can be used as soap.

Young waterbuck

Kudu bull browsing

Steenbuck (male). Harry Kirkman's favourite.

Scrub hare. Only seen at night when they emerge from the grass cover to feed. A common sight as they run in front of the vehicles, frightened by the lights and their own shadows.

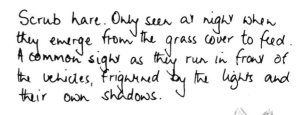

Busy little person of the night.

Lion heads. Backview shows the dark patches behind the ears which help the animals communicate with one another.

Mother and child

Old "daga" (mud) boy; rejected by the herd, old buffalo gents such as this one, usually form into pairs, spending their retirement rolling in the warm mud, chewing the cud, waiting for the end.

Common or Grey duiker.

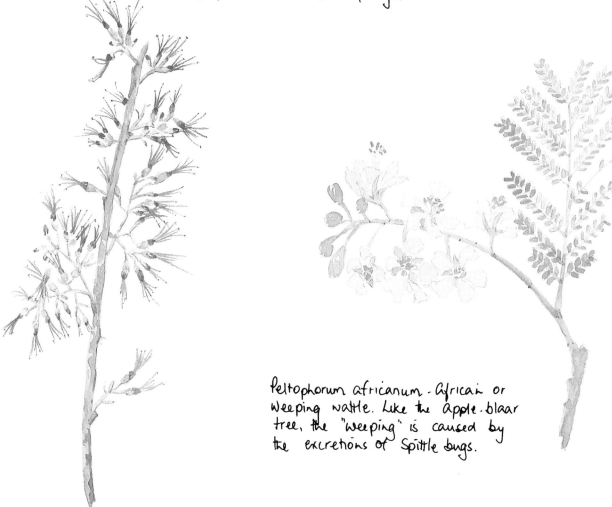

Flame creeper, festooned over the bush
beside the river near Harry's.

Peltophorum africanum - African or
Weeping wattle. Like the apple-blaar
tree, the "weeping" is caused by
the excretions of spittle bugs.

African or Weeping wattle (Peltophorum africanum) are beginning to appear. This tree's common name arises from the activities of spittle bugs (Ptyelus grossus) who, while feeding on the sap of the twigs, exude a watery 'spittle' which drips from the tree like rain. The Apple-leaf tree (Lonchocarpus capassa) is also visited by the spittle bugs in the springtime. In the camp, large pendulant blooms hang strangely upside-down from the Sausage trees, and beside the reception office the Impala lilies, which in winter bore bright white and red star-flowers, now bear velvety pink horns, which are the fascinating seed-pods

Velvety pods of the Impala lily.
(Reduced by 50%.)

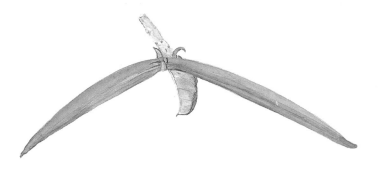

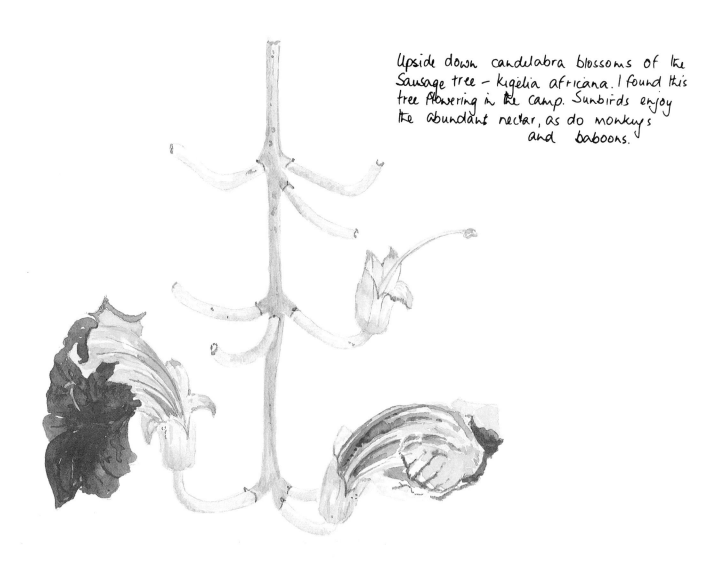

Upside down candelabra blossoms of the Sausage tree – kigelia africana. I found this tree flowering in the camp. Sunbirds enjoy the abundant nectar, as do monkeys and baboons.

Once the rain falls the bushveld is miraculously transformed. Almost overnight the burnt areas become as green as English fields, a magnet to all the grazers. Warthogs use their tough snouts to bulldoze huge troughs in the soft earth, to get at roots and other delicacies which the hard winter soil had hidden from them. The thick grasses of the bush – Themeda, Panicum and Aristida – send up tender green shoots.

We watch an old elephant bull rip up great tufts of soft new Buffalo grass beside the river road. First a tug, then a flip back and the soft lips at the end of the trunk grab the grass and put it into his gaping mouth.

67

African hoopoe - its bill adapted to probe the earth for insects and worms.

Yellow-billed hornbill

Bennett's woodpecker. One of the four species of woodpeckers found at Malamala. The bird makes holes in the bark with its sharp beak, inserting its long sticky tongue to extract insects.

Leopard tortoise ~ going along at his own slow pace in front of our land-rover.

Female mantid.

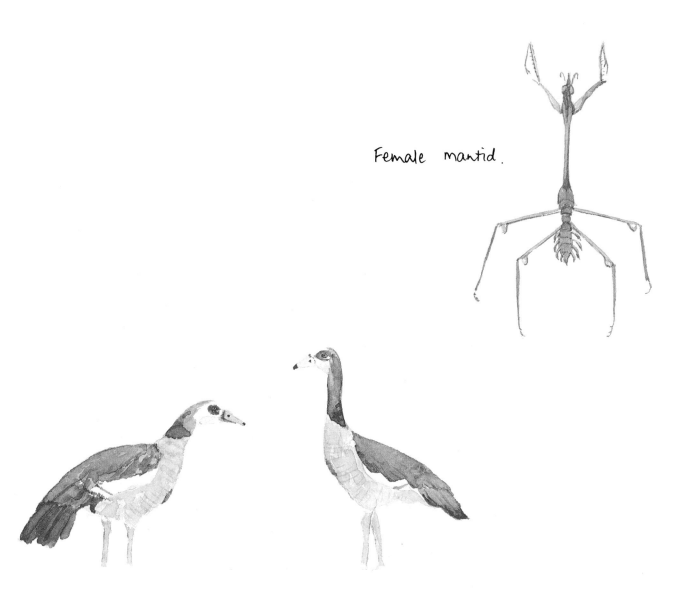

Pair of Egyptian geese

Short-horned pyrgomorphid grasshopper (male)

He cannot see down his trunk what he is eating, the selection is made by feel and smell. He munches contentedly, taking little notice of our presence.

Giraffe are feeding off the tender new leaves of the Buffalo thorn trees (Ziziphus mucronata). They have no incisors on their long upper jaws, but have a hard pad which, with their long, tough tongues, enables them to strip the leaves from the branches, undeterred by the wickedly sharp thorns. These same thorns seem to reach out for us as we drive through the bush following a magnificent maned lion, who pads along unconcernedly, leaving his footprints on the dewy grass. The thorns plague him too – he stops and with his teeth pulls a thorny twig from the pad of his right foot. Head low on the ground, he sniffs at grass and bushes as he passes, apparently on the war path. (Our ranger's diagnosis of the situation was correct, as that night the lion found a rival male for whom he was searching and a noisy fight ensued, the battle sound echoing mightily from across the river). The lion's roar, emitted by our friend a few metres away from us, is incredibly loud and grand, sending shivers through us, as we sit silently and in awe in our open vehicle, wondering what will happen next.

North of Campbell koppies, we stop to admire the flowers of the trailing Marama bean (Tylosema fassoglense). Nearby we notice a dear little biscuit-coloured giraffe, looking surprisingly like an ostrich, as he sits, head up, in the short green grass. He staggers to his feet as we approach, and walks slowly and with quaint dignity towards his mother's side.

In the road is something on a much smaller scale: a pair of dung beetles (Scarabs) are taking advantage not only of a large clump of rhino dung, but of the soft state of the earth. Their dung food ball, almost the size of a golf ball, is being rolled across the road from the patch of dung where it presumably was made. The male beetle (about 2 centimetres in length) pushes the ball with his back legs while his mate sits atop the ball, having to adjust her stance continually (rather like a circus performer) only just avoiding being squashed as the ball rolls. Perhaps her function is to give directions to her mate labouring below, as there

Two Dung beetles rolling their ball. was the beetle on top giving directions?

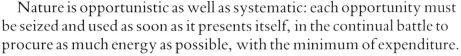

Tylosema fassoglense - Marama bean.
Trailing in the new grass north of
Campbell koppies.

seems no way that he can know where he is
going! As he pushes the ball up the incline
from the road, an intruder appears. The
invading dung beetle immediately climbs
aboard the dung-ball. In a flash papa beetle
dashes over and with the skill of a black-
belt karate expert, and using the flat edge
of his head, he flips the intruder on to its back.
The intruder scrambles to his feet and comes
into the attack again, and again is flipped
over. The female beetle on the ball takes
no part in the action. After several
unsuccessful onslaughts (which all end
with its legs in the air) the invader
moves off in the opposite direction,
perhaps to find its own ball or mate, or both.

Nature is opportunistic as well as systematic: each opportunity must
be seized and used as soon as it presents itself, in the continual battle to
procure as much energy as possible, with the minimum of expenditure.

Early on a spring afternoon drive, after the rain had soaked the earth
some nights previously, winged termites emerged from their nest.
Usually this emergence takes place at sunset when the chances of
survival of the pioneering pairs is greater. We watched a Steppe eagle
(recently returned from wintering in Asia or Europe) guzzling the
insects as they streamed from their hole. He seemed to dance on the
ground, (somewhat like a hen scratching for grubs) as he grabbed at this
providential supply of protein. Soon he was joined by a host of other
birds of prey: Lesser spotted eagles, Wahlberg's eagle, Bateleurs and a
Black kite, dipped and swooped after the insects.

This is the beginning of the breeding season for the korhaans. We
watched a Black-bellied korhaan performing his courtship display. First
he uttered his piercing call, head up, neck stretched; then he suddenly
rose high into the air, tumbling back to earth, coming out of his free-fall
just in time.

71

Pill millipede - awake   and asleep

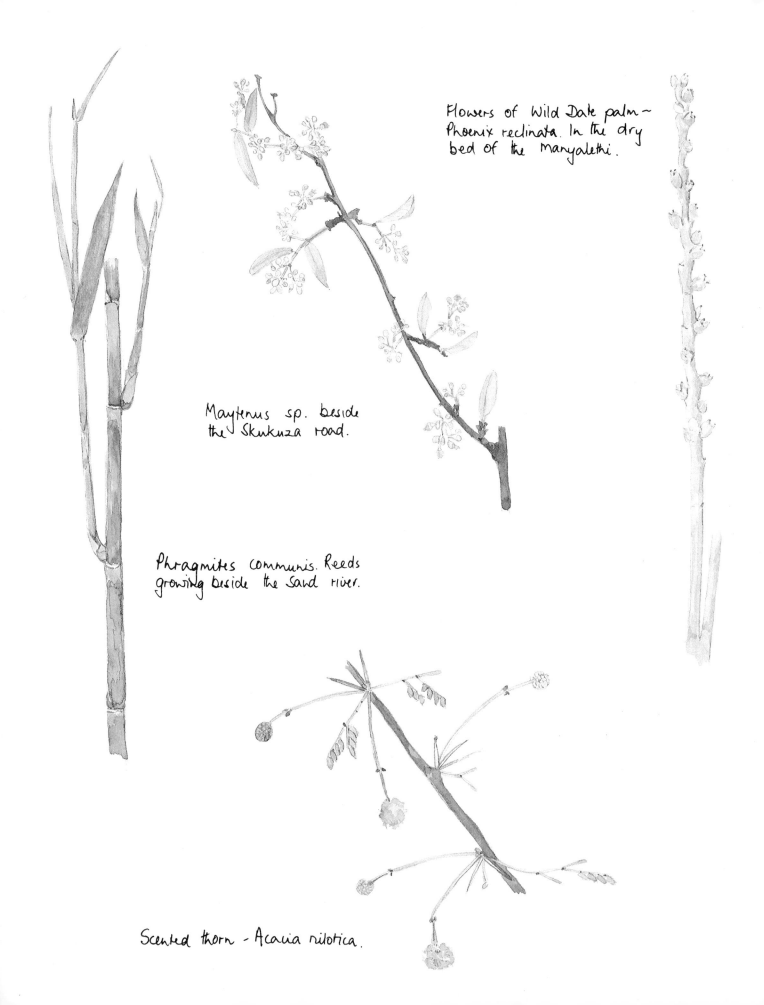

Flowers of Wild Date palm ~
Phoenix reclinata. In the dry
bed of the Manyalethi.

Maytenus sp. beside
the Skukuza road.

Phragmites communis. Reeds
growing beside the Sand river.

Scented thorn - Acacia nilotica.

Flower of Long-tailed cassia –
Cassia abbreviata. The pods
are 80cm long and take almost
a year to ripen.

Cassine species.

New leaves of
Silver-leafed terminalia.

At the Hippo pool, where the Sand river is wide, deep and slow-flowing, a congregation of hippos lie placidly in the brown water, only the tops of their great heads and parts of their fat backs showing. Little pink-lined ears, and bulging eyes protrude from their hairless heads. There is a constant rising and falling of their great bodies. There is a song which, while not factually correct, we sang as children … it goes:

> The hip-hip-hippopotamus
> he can beat the lot of us
> he can stay, so they say
> u–n–d–e–r the w–a–t–e–r for half-a-day!

When the sun sets they will emerge to feed on the grassy river bank. Hippos eat about 130 kilograms of grass a day. It is not warm enough for the resident crocodile to sun himself on his accustomed rock to the west of the hippo pool; no doubt he is lurking somewhere in the cool depths of the river.

Sunset colours in the spring tend to pinks and lavenders, rather than the dramatic oranges of the dust-laden winter skies. Now the air is clear,

Lesser Galago –
Nagapie. Caught
in the glare of
our spotlight.

Hippo pool on a late spring afternoon.

Spotted Eagle owl.
Their eerie call can
often be heard in the
night at camp.

Pearl-spotted owl.

which seems to give the stars an extra sparkle as they appear in the velvet sky.

At night the frogs take over the music making from the birds, as they call raucously to their mates. Passing through Mlowathi stream there is a marvellous chorus of Reedfrogs, Rattling and Bubbling frogs, Puddle frogs, Ranas and Foam Nest frogs. At this time of year the foam nests of the latter are attached to branches which overhang pools and waterpans. These nests are made co-operatively of a foam secreted by several mating pairs of Tree frogs (Chiromantis xerampelina). Into the still moist foam the eggs are deposited. About five days later the eggs hatch and the tadpoles drop into the water below, there to undergo the final stage of their metamorphosis.

At Piccadilly pans the frog noise is almost deafening. Joining the gutteral and piping harmony is the beautiful birdlike trill of the Red-banded frog (Phyrnomerus bifasciatus). Near the old air strip, where water lies boggy in great marshy areas, Giant Pyxie bullfrogs add their whooping contribution from the shallow water.

Sitting in the grass at the edge of the airstrip is an adult female leopard. Like any respectable member of the feline race, she performs her toilet: her neck arches as she cleans the front of her chest; she rubs her whiskers with her paws, scratches and yawns. She appears not to be bothered by our flashlight which plays upon her marvellous spotted body. After a while she rises and with supple grace walks beside and

Phrynobatrachus
natalensis - Snoring
puddle-frog.

75

Female long-horned grasshopper
or katydid!

Foam nest frog -
with toes like "E.T."!

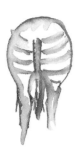

Gonimbrasia belina ♀ Mopane moth.

past us, her velvet coat rippling and almost silvery in the light from the vehicle.

Spring evenings at camp are filled with myriad sounds and smells: the sweet fragrance of the knob-thorn flowers scents the air; there are the calls of crickets and frogs; the Fiery-necked nightjar entreats 'Good Lord deliver us'; a pair of Scops owls exchange purring trills. Other creatures are communicating silently and secretly; two beige and orange Emperor moths have somehow found one another and mate on the lawn beside the diningroom. There is a sense of bursting life and fecundity in the tropical night air.

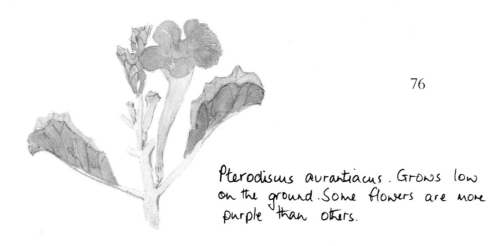

Pterodiscus aurantiacus. Grows low on the ground. Some flowers are more purple than others.

THE CAMPBELL YEARS: 1927-1964
THE PLEASURE OF THIS PLACE

William Alfred Campbell, known throughout his life as 'Wac', was born in 1880 on Cornubia, a sugar estate in the Mount Edgecombe area, north of Durban in Natal. His mother, Ellen, was the daughter of John Blamey, a well-known sugar farmer who had emigrated from Cornwall in 1850; his father, Marshall, was at the time of Wac's birth, struggling to buy Cornubia, which he managed. With the help of a Durban financier, Marshall later became the owner of the estate, which was the first step on the ladder which he rapidly climbed to great heights in the Natal sugar industry. Soon he became a director on the board of the Natal Central Sugar Company, and he and his family moved to a new home – Mount Edgecombe House – where Wac and his siblings grew up.

Marshall's father, William, had emigrated from Scotland under the Byrne Settler scheme in 1850. After years of hardship, during which he helped to build the north pier of Durban's bay, William saved sufficient money to buy land at Umhloti, where he pioneered sugar farming, and imported the first sugar crushing machinery in South Africa. Both Wac's grandfather and father were men of public spirit and vision; had Grandfather William not died at an early age, his contribution to his adopted land might have been even greater; Marshall not only rose to the top in the sugar industry, but in 1898 was elected to the Natal Legislative Council in the Crown Colony Administration. Later he represented the Natal Coast in the Upper House of the Natal Parliament and, after Union in 1910, was elected a senator in the new Parliament (despite the fact that he had refused to sign the act of Union because the 'natives' had not been consulted). Marshall was knighted for his services to his country. A man much loved and respected by the black people of Natal, he had the unique honour of being a counsellor of the black

77

Amaqedi tribe (a position which his son Wac held after Marshall's death). A large black settlement north of Durban is named in his honour: KwaMashu – the place of Marshall.

Wac's uncle, Marshall's brother Sam, was a distinguished medical doctor and benefactor, responsible for starting the first technical college in Natal, as well as the Child Welfare Society. Like his brother he was interested in the political issues of the day, having also the Campbell gift of putting pen with ease to paper, a gift which was manifested most notably in Sam's son, the illustrious South African poet, Roy Campbell. Wac's sister Killie was to make her mark as an antiquarian and

78

Killie and Wac at the turn of the century.
(Killie Campbell Museum)

Killie and her cousin
Roy, the poet

(Killie Campbell Museum)

benefactress of distinction. On her death in 1965 she left her library of
thousands of volumes of carefully accumulated Africana to Natal
University, an institution of which her cousin George was at one time
the Chancellor.

Wac – 'Mfo-ka-Mashu', as he was called by the Zulus, 'son of
Marshall' – was educated at Hilton College in Natal, and at Cambridge
University. He served as a captain in the Natal Mounted Rifles during
the Bambatha Rebellion in 1906, and during the 1914–1918 war acted as
a Marine Landing Officer. He was also ADC to the Governor of Natal,
Sir Matthew Nathan. From 1906 he had been employed at the Natal
Estates, starting as his father before him, at the bottom of the ladder.

At the end of the First War, Wac was suffering from extremely poor
health, and was persuaded by an old friend of the family to get out into
the wilds of Zululand and do some hunting. This family friend was old

Wac in the uniform of
the Natal Mounted Rifles.
(Killie Campbell Museum)

Frank Fynney – "Logoza" – "the old vermin hunter", with a trapped leopard at Hluhluwe.
(Campbell family)

Frank Fynney. Frank was born in 1857 of parents who had been passengers on the brig *Conquering Hero* which brought William Campbell and his wife to Durban in 1850, and the families had remained close friends. 'Uncle' Frank had always been a hunter and lover of the wilds: Wac claimed that Fynney had taught the famous Selous all the latter knew of hunting. 'Logoza' (by which name Fynney was always known), was the name the Zulus gave him, being their word (*–lokoza*) for 'dimly visible', which referred to the fact that Fynney always sat in the smoke of the campfire, as he maintained that this prevented him from being bitten by mosquitoes; it also made his eyes perpetually red. Logoza's hunting grounds were in the wild areas of the Umfolosi and Hluhluwe valleys; there is a railway siding in Zululand called Logoza, which honours his name.

It was during those first hunting days that Wac met another character who loved the bush, who would become Wac's dearest and lifelong friend. Alec Logan (called 'Makaleek' by the Zulus) was, at the time

81

Wac first met him, farming in a small way in the Hluhluwe area. Logan's father had been a transport rider in the 1860s, taking dynamite and, of all things, ceiling boards, by ox-wagon from Durban to the gold-mining town of Barberton. Old Logan would return by ship from the port at Delagoa Bay, while his trusted Zulu assistant returned with the oxen and wagons by road, a round trip which took six months. Alec Logan's first 'residence', in the remote bush of Natal, was a few sheets of corrugated iron propped against a thorn tree. This little home, it was said, he shared with two hyenas, a couple of pigs and innumerable dogs. This unlikely and motley assembly of four-footed friends followed Logan everywhere, even on his frequent visits to the Hluhluwe post office. Perhaps the sight of the young man trailed by this strange but faithful retinue helped to endear him to the postmistress, for she subsequently married him.

Thus Wac, in the winter of 1916, accompanied by Frank Fynney, set out by train, and was met at the railhead, Somkele, by Alec Logan, complete with donkey cart. The party embarked on the first of many such hunting trips into the Umfolosi area. This was the start not only of Wac's enduring love of hunting, but also the beginning of years of robust health.

By the mid 1920s Wac's interest in wild life and its management and conservation had led to his appointment, in 1926, as the Natal representative on the newly constituted National Parks Board. A fellow member, HB Papenfus, invited Wac to stay with him on the TCL's farm Toulon, which adjoined the Kruger Park. This was Wac's first experience of the magic of the Transvaal lowveld. He was evidently immediately under its spell, for in a letter dated August 27 1927, he thanked Papenfus for the 'glorious little holiday', adding that for him it was a 'red-letter day' as he had decided to buy land in that area. He hoped Papenfus would be a guest on his game farm once he had purchased it.

Wac's father-in-law, George Armstrong, who had Eastern Transvaal connections, as his father had been a pioneer gold miner in the Barberton area in the 1880s, also thought that as the Zululand hunting

82

grounds were becoming 'shot out', pastures new should be found. What better place than the land recently made available through the consolidation of the Kruger Park?

The previous year two Johannesburg men had the same idea: Charles Varty and Frank Unger had purchased the farm Sparta from the TCL, becoming the first people to buy land in the area solely for the purpose of being able to enjoy the game.

Logan had by this time joined Natal Estates, his farming venture having failed, and Wac arranged for him to inspect the farm Eyrefield which was being offered for sale at 12/6d a morgen. The TCL ranger, Tomlinson, was acting as agent on behalf of the owner, a Mr Hurd. Wac considered the purchase price of £2 150 12 6d reasonable, provided there was water and, of course, game.

(Both Logan and Tomlinson were under the impression that Eyrefield was on the Sand river, and it was only after Wac had bought the farm and had it surveyed by a member of his staff, that it was discovered that it was not Eyrefield but MalaMala through which the river ran).

'Dear Mr Campbell,…' Logan wrote on September 19 1927, 'Attached please find an estimate of the game to be found on the farm Eyrefield'. He had found small game scarce, but reported that the most abundant species were Wildebeest (300), Impala (600), and Sable Antelope (200). He had observed that vermin were numerous and would have to be reduced. 'If it should be my luck to go up…' he continued, he would be pleased to give instructions in the use of traps. Before he ended the letter (with the words 'Yours respectfully'), he thanked Wac for 'the pleasant trip and your very fine generosity to me'. Until his death from cancer twenty-six years later, it *was* to be Logan's luck to 'go up' each winter, where he became the most indispensable member of Wac's annual bushveld safari.

Wac wrote to Tomlinson thanking him for helping Logan and asked him to secure the services of a reliable 'native' game guard for Eyrefield, a person Wac wanted 'sworn in'. Wac would send him a badge to wear. He also asked Tomlinson to arrange for a stockade and a cottage to be built beside the Sand river. He enclosed a sketch of both buildings, and

83

suggested that they be built on a spot which Logan had suggested 'just where you and he jumped off your horses to climb up the Kopje to look at the Beacon. In any case', he added, 'use your own discretion, and as this is close to the boundary of "Marthly" please see we are not landed'. Wac asked in the same letter if Tomlinson would 'find out about Marthly and MalaMala…'.

Two months later Wac signed the Deed of Sale and paid the first instalment of the purchase price of MalaMala. The price paid was 20 shillings a morgen, a total of £3 656 6s 6d. Transfer was however, only effected in May 1929. In an excited letter written to the Transvaal Provincial Secretary, Wac explained that his intention in purchasing the farms was 'the strict preservation of game with the object of handing this on as a legacy to my youngsters when I get old'.

Tomlinson must have used his own discretion in finding a site of build Wac's first camp. He chose a lovely area where the Mlowathi stream flows into the Sand river, which is some distance from the foot of the hill on which a beacon stands. The buildings which were made of knob-thorn poles, the roofs thatched roughly with reeds from the river, were in fact constructed by a young man who had recently come to the area.

Harry Kirkman had been at Toulon when Alec Logan arrived on his mission to investigate the possibility of Wac's purchasing Eyrefield. Kirkman had arrived in June of that year to take over the post of TCL ranger from Tomlinson who was leaving to become a ranger in the Kruger Park. Tomlinson had arranged to remain at Toulon for some months to show Harry the ropes. Kirkman recalls that it was during this time of probation that he helped Tomlinson rebuild an old Boer War wagon which Tomlinson had found on MalaMala. They used local acacia wood, but on completion of their task found that the wagon was so heavy that it needed at least ten oxen to pull it. Tomlinson had to leave for the Park using his old Scotch cart.

Harry Kirkman had his time cut out protecting the TCL cattle from predators, and many are the stories he tells of his adventures shooting the lions who found the kraaled cattle a far easier prey than the swift-moving antelope. During the six years of his cattle management, Harry Kirkman dispatched over 500 lions. Not that shooting the lion was easy: many where the nights when he sat up alone in a thorn tree, the lower half of his body encased in a grain sack for warmth, an ordinary two-cell flashlight screwed to the barrel of his gun, waiting for lion to come to the bait he had placed. Fortunately Harry was a fine shot. Once he accounted for twenty-five lion in seven consecutive nights; his record for a single session was eight. Close to his house at Toulon he shot five lions in one night. Harry is quick explain that this wasn't 'hunting', and that he shot only to carry out instructions, which he did with responsibility and great skill. Harry didn't mess about: his first shot was the one that counted. Using a .303 rifle, he could fire an accurate head-shot up to sixty yards.

Harry lived simply and contentedly, alone in the house at Toulon which the TCL had built, listening to the calls of the bush at night: zebra, kudu, impala, and of course, lion. Sometimes the bellowing of the cattle in the nearby kraals interrupted the bush noises, signifying an attack by predators. The cattle kraals were built of stout knob-thorn poles embedded in the ground, around which dried thorn branches were piled. At the kraal's entrance was a hut in which the herd boys slept. At the sound of lion approaching, burning brands of wood would be flung out at the would-be intruders.

So Harry spent his days, alone, but out in the bush where he was happiest. There was, however, paper work which he was obliged to do, but which he hated. In the old files of the TCL there is a letter from Kirkman to Percy Greathead, the land manager, in reply to the latter's enquiry regarding confusion with beacons on some of the properties. Harry wrote: 'I should have written to you before about this lot, but ye gods I have enough writing to do in this bally office...'.

Harry looked forward to the winter months as they meant the advent of some of the farm owners, and brought a welcome change to his routine of caring for the Company's 2 500 head of cattle. It was expected of him to help the owners as much as possible. In those early days he remembers only Arthur (of the farm Gowrie, at the north of the block), Varty, Unger and Wac, coming to visit their farms. Harry would meet the visitors at the Toulon siding (on the Selati line), and help with transport to the various camps. He enjoyed the novelty of having company in that wide wilderness. While Wac was in camp, Harry frequently rode to MalaMala for supper in the evening, delighting in the yarns which the visitors told around the camp fire in the boma, and of course adding some stories of his own. Then he would saddle up and ride the dark lonely road home. Today he looks back on those days with nostalgia: 'They were a fine bunch of chaps', he says.

In May 1928 Wac applied for permits to shoot game on his farms. He apparently felt obliged to explain to the magistrate at Pilgrim's Rest that while he had bought the farms as a shooting box, he was also an 'ardent Game protectionist and not a Biltong Hunter'. He added that in the past he had furnished various museums with specimens of game and birds from his Natal estates, and hoped to continue this practice at MalaMala. At that time the only species of 'open' game were kudu, waterbuck, zebra and sassaby. Vermin (which included all of the carnivores) could be shot without a permit.

In the winter of that year Wac, his father-in-law George Armstrong, and a few pals, including Frank Fynney and Logan, with Taffy Boyce (from the Durban museum), set off on the long, arduous journey by train to the lowveld, to inspect the properties for the first time. A cattle truck was loaded at Mount Edgecombe with provisions: half a dozen gun dogs, eight horses, eighteen servants (headed by Wac's faithful Mhlaba), tents, saddles, food and cooking equipment. The hunters joined the train that Monday evening at Durban station, and after changes at Pretoria and Komatipoort (at the latter they had an interminable wait before being transferred on to the Selati line), they arrived at Toulon siding at midday on Thursday, only to find that the 'impendimenta' had not arrived. The horses, servants and provisions were eventually traced to Acornhoek, and arrived the following day. Harry Kirkman helped the weary hunters (understandly exhausted after their uncomfortable three days in the train) to get to their campsite, with the aid of his buckboard and mules. They followed the trail through the

The first Malamala campsite : 1928/1929

(Campbell family)

bush which the sledges of the resident blacks had worn, as the old three-sided conveyances were dragged along the ground by oxen.

That first camp was more a reconnaissance than a hunting party; the men only had three weeks' leave, a great deal of which was to be spent in travelling. Despite the brevity of the time, Frank Fynney trapped: thirty-one wild dogs, six civet cats, four genet cats, four hyenas and one leopard. No wonder Wac called 'Uncle' Frank the 'old vermin hunter'. It became evident to Wac that there was some confusion regarding the boundaries of the farm, and he hurriedly sent for William Paul, the General Manager of Natal Estates. Paul was a qualified surveyor, and he, with the help of other members of the party, discovered that their camp was not on Eyrefield, but on MalaMala. George Armstrong was also in for a shock: he found that he had bought the farm Ravenscourt believing it to be Marthly! These were not the only confusions of identity regarding the farms. Two years before, J Arthur, the owner of Gowrie, was spending his third annual winter holiday hunting on his farm, when he was apprehended by the police who informed him that he was trespassing. Arthur begged the policeman *please* to show him where Gowrie was, as he had been looking for it for the past three years. (The Arthurs had visited the bushveld for the first time in 1923, riding horses they had brought with them on the train from Heidelberg to their campsite – which was on the river – probably near where MalaMala camp is today. During the month all but one of the horses died of horsesickness. Arthur's young son was sent to ride alone to Toulon to ask ranger Tomlinson for the loan of his mules and buckboard, so that they could return to catch the train at Toulon siding. Recalling the event forty-four years later, Arthur wrote in 1967: 'I was dead scared as we had trouble every night with lions at camp'.)

On 5 July 1928, Wac sent a three-page telegram to his wife from Acornhoek. It read:

> More than satisfied with my purchase stop All in camp enthusiastic stop Feel I did the right thing in following you my mother and your father's advice stop I wish the staff to feel they have a common interest with us in the pleasure of this place so that each year they will have something to look forward to stop Tell our sons they must come up in a year or so stop Very comfortable rondavels situated alongside beautiful river stop Delightful climate stop Game varied and numerous saw two cheetah chasing waterbuck stop George got his lion stop All well love stop Please communicate to staff through Masters address Campbell Acornhoek. William.

Another telegram was despatched to Mrs Campbell from William Paul:

> Unanimous vote of thanks passed at our first Camp fire for your influence in purchase of the farms which are affording us extreme pleasure stop We appreciate deeply the pleasure of being able to share the pleasure this place affords stop Far surpasses our expectations stop

Teeming with Game as I have had ample opportunity of investigating while picking out beacons stop Would be grateful if you would communicate this to the staff through Masters stop Nights extremely cold stop Water frozen in the morning all well. Paul.

There was no doubt that the farms were living up to everyone's expectations, and Wac who had bought them not only for his pleasure but for that of the employees of Natal Estates, the company of which he had become the Managing Director that year, was more than delighted.

The following year Wac and party again entrained for MalaMala, with slightly less impedimenta – the eight horses had been left at Toulon in the care of Harry Kirkman. The camp was still on the other side of the river and the guests were carried through the river on the backs of the trackers. One of the members of that camp of 1929 is still alive and recalls that the camp consisted of a few huts and a central tent, which, writes AG ('Monty') Brickhill, 'was always well-stocked with big sweet navel oranges'. According to Monty Brickhill, the other members in

Where the navel oranges were stored. 1929
(Campbell family)

camp were: Wac's sons Athol and Urban, Frank Brickhill (Monty's father who was foreman of the mill), Frank Fynney, Alec Logan, Taffy Boyce (from the Durban museum), Harold Millar, André (Wac's driver), a German Count, and Boboza, Wac's deaf and dumb cook who, with Mhlaba, kept the sixteen servants and the camp itself in order.

Good rains had fallen that year, so the game was scattered. Several exciting events were recorded. A trapped leopard was shot, the shot missed the leopard but released the trap. Kehla, an old black tracker, dispatched the leopard by hitting it on the head with his knobkerrie. Mr PE Masters (also of the Sugar Estates) had built himself a 'machan' in a large ebony tree at a waterhole on Marthly. In order to facilitate his climb into the tree he had driven steel spikes into the tree's trunk. That night, as Masters sat alone in his tree, a lioness, who had cubs with her, attempted to jump into the tree after Masters, leaving some of her fur behind on the steel stakes.

That year Wac's younger son Urban, then a lad of eleven years, was taken by Frank Fynney to shoot a Wild dog which had been caught in one of Fynney's traps. The animal had broken all its teeth on the steel trap and was whimpering when they got there. At this distressing sight, the lad not surprisingly burst into tears. In a memoir Urban wrote in later years, he described the incident, recalling that Logoza (Fynney) and his father were disgusted at his softheartedness. Wac instructed Fynney to 'keep him at it – he's got to get used to it'.

It was very near the site of Wac's first camp that the 'Kruger Millions' were said to have been hidden. During the Boer War, President Kruger had taken the Transvaal Republic's gold reserve (much in the form of sovereigns) with him as he retreated from the British towards the Eastern Transvaal. Legend has it that the gold sovereigns were secreted somewhere in the lowveld. Through the years countless treasure seekers have searched fruitlessly for the missing millions. Stevenson-Hamilton wrote that in the early days of the Sabi Game Reserve, he watched many treasure hunters set off for the banks of the Sand river, with shovels and high hopes, only to return empty-handed. Wac's guests were aware of the legend, but there is no record of anyone taking the rumour seriously;

Crossing the Sand river
to the first campsite.
1928
(Campbell family)

Dr George Campbell, Wac's cousin, with the first lion shot
at Malamala. 1929

Wac's "Queen Mary",
with happy hunters
aboard.

(Campbell family)

they were far too happy and occupied with hunting for game rather than
gold.

From the first time that Wac camped on his farms he sent meticulous
game reports to the magistrate at Pilgrim's Rest, reports that were
greatly appreciated. Alec Logan was responsible for editing the reports;
Parfitt, who was Wac's 'scribe' typed them. Not only were the
numbers, weights and measurements of each animal shot, recorded, but
Wac included observations regarding the weather, the state of the grass
and bush, and any unusual or exciting occurrences.

In 1930 the camp was moved to its present site, on the near side of the
river, as it was felt that it would be easier not to ford the river to get to
camp. Using a similar plan and construction as that used in the Kruger
Park, four rondavels were built from concrete, with thatched roofs, as
well as two bathrooms, one of which abutted on to the kitchen. Some

92

wattle and daub huts were also built, which served as store-rooms and additional accommodation. One of these was given for the sole use of Taffy Boyce who, besides having to store a great deal of museum paraphenalia, was also a radio 'ham'. Apart from the strange smells of preserving fluids which emanated from Taffy's hut, were trailing wires from radio aerials, which he strung on to a large tree above his roof. The hut became known as 'Marconi House'. A 500 gallon (2 000 litre) tank on a high stand stored water which was hand-pumped from the Sand river. Water for the kitchen and bathrooms was heated in a forty-four gallon drum, the fire being continuously fed with wood gathered in the bush. Fortunately the supply of fuel was unending, as the appetite of this antiquated but efficient scheme was prodigious. This system was updated when a boiler was designed and installed later by Fred Macbeth, the Chief Engineer of Natal Estates. This boiler was used for twenty years, and now stands in sad and rusty retirement behind the present

93

camp, a memorial to those more primitive days).

The camp 'loos' were two old-fashioned 'long-drops', built side-by-side, screened by a fence of reeds both from each other and the bush behind. Leading to the 'loos' was a reed passageway, long enough (as a former guest explained) to enable anyone in the 'loo' to 'give a discreet cough to indicate occupancy'. The 'loos' were close enough together so that if one so desired one could chat to the person in the other loo. One old-timer recalls passing the time of day with the Earl of Clarendon as he responded to nature's call in the winter of '35. A former (female) guest remembers that she visited the loo with some apprehension, always expecting to be interrupted by wild animals bursting through the reeds.

The boma, where the evening meal was eaten, was a circle of tall reeds built beneath the giant jakalsbessie tree, where it still stands today.

(Old Madala Jim, one of the two police 'boys' recruited by Wac in 1927, had laid prior claim to this splendid tree, and had his kraal beneath it. When Wac moved camp from across the river. Madala Jim had to move house). In the boma, guests sat around a huge fire of leadwood logs (which is the wood that has been used for lowveld campfires throughout the ages), at small tables which were the boxes in which tins of paraffin had been packed. Taffy Boyce was responsible for the design of their conversion. (These wooden boxes were also, incidentally, used in other ways in the camp, both as tables in the rondavels, and as shelves for clothes). In 1960 it was decided to make the tables higher and wider for the convenience of adults, the original tables being kept for the use of children. These same post-1960 tables are still being used in the MalaMala boma.

The routine of the camp was laid down from the first, both in respect

Princess Alice with her lion. July 1930. Tayi Mhlambo is on her right; the gallant Alec Logan on her left. (Photograph kindly loaned by Mrs J. Briscoe, Alec Logan's daughter)

of camp procedure and of hunting. Guests were required to be back in camp by sunset; permits had to be signed immediately an animal was shot, to avoid misunderstandings with game-patrols; the hunter had to have his tracker with him at all times; guns must be unloaded *outside* huts (the state of the walls of some of the rondavels indicated that this instruction was not always obeyed); only solitary bulls were to be shot except in the case of wildebeest and zebra; vermin could be shot without permits; Wild dogs should be shot on sight. No animals, except lion, should be shot on the camp side of the river, or in the area opposite the

96

camp for a mile on either side, and for the same distance inland; this area was regarded as a sanctuary, so that guests in camp might watch game coming to the river to drink.

There is an amusing letter in the files of the TCL which the Company wrote to Harry Kirkman, stating that Mr Campbell had complained that the Company's dogs (which were in fact dogs owned by black employees) were interfering with his game. In future, therefore, the TCL instructed, no dogs with legs 'longer than four inches' were permitted to be in the possession of the blacks.

This letter also alerted Kirkman to the fact that South Africa's Governor-General and his wife were to visit MalaMala in the coming winter. 1930 was an auspicious year for Wac, due to the visit of his first 'notable' guests (a trend that would continue for the rest of Wac's ownership of MalaMala). Princess Alice, a granddaughter of Queen Victoria, and her husband the Earl of Athlone, together with their daughter Lady May Cambridge, and members of their entourage, had expressed their desire to visit MalaMala in the winter of that year. Wac had planned to stay in the lowveld through the winter months until the viceregal party arrived; however a note arrived from a representative of the Board of Directors of Natal Estates, conveying the message that a large number of shareholders in England considered Campbell's 'continued absence during the crushing season' inadvisable. Wac had to return to work for a week and dash back to MalaMala to meet his important guests.

Telegrams and letters connected with the proposed visit flew back and forth. Wac explained the route the party should take to the farm, and described the accommodation they would find when they got there: 'the buildings consist of four large rondavels twenty foot in diameter' he wrote, 'in which there are beds and mattresses sufficient for a party of twenty-four. On the arrival of the party arrangements as to accommodation could be made to suit the Princess...'.

Wac arranged for the required hunting permits. He wrote to Harry Kirkman asking him to assist 'as a huntsman', as Wac found the visit 'a big responsibility' and would be relying on Kirkman 'to help (me) a lot'.

97

He wrote also to one of his employees who was already installed at MalaMala informing him that he required 'two fat oxen from Kirkman to be killed in their honour'.

The viceregal party was a great success. Lions were plentiful. Her Royal Highness, who had Logan as a 'companion', tracked a lioness for some time before getting it in her sights. Finding that the Princess was trembling slightly from nervousness, Logan gallantly stretched out his arm so that she was able to rest her gun on it when she fired. The animal, unfortunately, was only wounded, and moved off on to the next door farm Sparta. Wac obtained permission to follow it, and the next day Logan and Kirkman tracked the wounded lioness and killed it.

The Athlones' four-day stay was memorable, the Princess recalling it with pleasure nearly fifty years later. Wac received a charming letter from the Princess, addressed to 'Dear Willie', thanking him for an 'absolutely glorious time'. Alec Logan, the Princess maintained, was 'a man in a thousand'. Wac in a subsequent letter to the Governor-General's ADC wrote that 'one and all of us have returned to our work feeling like a dog that has two tails'. Evidently the white members of the party were

The "Queen Mary" beneath the great Jakkalsbessie tree, which still shades the centre of malamala camp.
(Campbell family)

The trek to Malamala on a cold winter's day. Somewhere between Natal and the lowveld.

(Campbell family)

not the only ones who were feeling jubilant at the happy conclusion of the Athlones' stay. In the same letter Wac added: 'Kehla, whom you have termed the camp ADC has been celebrating the Princess' lioness with evident gusto. His wives have been brewing him copious supplies of beer and he is at present 'non est'. He will probably be himself again in a about a week's time'. So a good time was had by all.

The area where Her Excellency shot her lioness was named the Princess Alice bush in honour of the event. The only shadow to cloud an otherwise bright year was the death of one of Wac's most splendid hunting dogs, Lutjie, who was transfixed on the horns of a Sable antelope, and died a few days later.

Each year Wac, friends, and members of his staff visited MalaMala in the winter months. Wac was as good as his word, ensuring that his employees did indeed 'share the pleasure of this place'. He generously provided guns for staff members if they had none of their own, and for years paid their fares to and from the lowveld.

Women were not frequent visitors to the camp. Wac's wife came to

MalaMala for the first time in 1935 when, according to her son Urban's
memoirs, she transformed the camp, planting the many bougainvilleas
which fifty years later are still a glory of colour, and a landmark from
the sky. She also supervised the construction of a thatched summerhouse
on the banks of the river under a large jackalsbessie tree, where guests
could sit in the cool shade and enjoy lunch and afternoon tea. Mrs
Campbell planted large areas of aloes, and the beautiful Impala lilies,
which are still such a feature of the MalaMala camp.

The same year that the bougainvillea were planted, MalaMala was
visited by the Earl of Clarendon, who had succeeded Athlone as
Governor-General. Lions were shot almost daily. His Excellency had
lost his eldest son, Lord Hyde, in a shooting accident some time

Construction of "Clarendon House" in preparation for the Vice-regal visit. 1935
(Mrs Kinsman)

Winter 1935: The Earl of Clarendon (hat on) in centre; Wac is on his right.

(Len Gric)

101

previously, so was understandably anxious regarding the safety of his second son, the Hon Nicholas Villiers. The latter was entrusted to the care of Len Grice, who took the young man out in Grice's two-seater, with Zaba, Wac's best tracker, sitting in the dicky seat. Young Villiers shot a lion with a good head shot. His father proved to be equally adept with a gun. Wac, as was his custom, despatched telegrams, one to his wife and one to his mother, Lady Campbell, recounting verbosely the hunting prowess of their Excellencies, and suggesting that the womenfolk should send congratulatory telegrams to the Governor-General by return of post.

There was a procedure following the shooting of a lion which was traditional and adhered to throughout Wac's time at MalaMala. A cry, the 'Campbell cry' – 'ngaulana', was uttered by Wac whenever a leopard or a lion was shot (no lesser beast warranted it). This cry it is said was the war-cry of an old Zulu regiment, and incidentally, became, subsequently, the name of Urban Campbell's home on the Natal coast. Someone on Toulon once had the temerity to yell 'Ngaulana' (fortunately not in Wac's hearing) and was *severely* reprimanded! '*The cry*' was permitted to be used by the trackers as they brought the lion carcass back to camp on the back of the specially-adapted jeep. Guests in camp would hear the cry, followed by the Shangaan 'lion song' as the procession crossed the river. Everyone, including the servants, would throng to the bridge. The 'natives' and their children armed themselves with sticks or reeds, and would form into a type of marching order, following the cavalcade as it moved slowly up the slope and into camp, the lion song being rendered all the while. The vehicle was driven beneath the huge tree from which hung a large Salter scale; the carcass would be weighed, measured, recorded, and of course photographed together with the victorious hunter. It was a time of praise and celebration: the Shangaans who lived year-round at MalaMala were always jubilant at the death of another of their enemies – the ingonyama.

That evening the successful hunter would have to recount to the assembled guests each detail of how he 'got' his lion; Wac would make a speech of congratulation, and everyone would drink to the huntsman.

Each time it was a real occasion: the hunter was well and truly 'lionized'.

In the first years traps were set around a lion kill, but this practice was discontinued when from experience it was learned that the lions frequently didn't return to their kill, and also that using traps could be a dangerous exercise. A more successful method was the use of bait, in the form of a whole or partial game carcass, which was placed in an area known to be frequented by lion. The hunter would sit up all night in a 'machan' in a tree, armed with torch and rifle, waiting for lion to make an appearance. Some hunters preferred to visit the baited spot at first light hoping for a shot at the lions before they left the kill. Many were the times when a lion was only wounded, and the huntsman would have to return to camp and ask for the help of additional trackers and dogs. Len Grice remembers that on his first hunting trip in 1931, using an inferior gun (which had cost him his full month's paycheck of £6) he wounded a lion. As Wac had not yet arrived from Mount Edgecombe,

103

Dr Nick Bodenstein with a 455 lb Sable antelope . July 1937
(Mrs M. Bodenstein)

Tracker Tayi Mhlambo in the 1930's.
(Len Grice)

Grice felt he should not borrow the dogs, so he and his tracker Tayi (who was to become Loring Rattray's chief ranger), rode over to Toulon to ask Harry Kirkman for help. From his bedroom, in which stood a cricket bat, a tennis racquet and a hold-all containing three guns, Harry selected a Mannlicher revolving-magazine rifle which Wac and the MalaMala hunters had given him the previous year, and loaded the rifle with five cartridges. 'Is that all you're taking?' enquired the amazed young Grice, indicating the ammunition. 'You said only *one* lion, didn't you?' replied Kirkman.

Grice was one of those hunters who usually went out on foot, accompanied by his tracker, spooring the king of beasts in daylight. This frequently involved flushing the lion out of thick bush which could be a hair-raising business, and required a good deal more courage than sitting up in the safety of a tree. Once the TCL discontinued their ranching activities and disposed of their cattle, the lion became less wary, and more hunters took to following lion on foot.

Each year the number of lion shot increased. In 1936 no less than eighteen lion were accounted for. Not all lion hunters were successful. That year one member of the party, who had sat up in the same tree for six consecutive nights without getting a shot at lion, decided to change his site. On arriving at his new tree at dusk ready for another night's vigil, he found that his tracker had not erected a 'machan' for him. Undaunted he managed with great effort to haul into the tree the seat of his car, and on this he spent a cold and uncomfortable night. Just before dawn he decided he had had enough, and climbed down from his eerie. From then on he hunted baboons instead.

Once the pont had been constructed across the Sabi river at Skukuza, visitors to MalaMala could travel by road which, although still arduous due to the rough condition of country roads in South Africa at that time, was less exhausting and time-consuming than travelling by train. From Natal, it was a car journey which necessitated two night stops, the first usually at Newcastle, the second at either Barberton or Nelspruit. Wac bought a large three-ton truck which was christened the Queen Mary, and this was sent up each winter in advance of the main party, filled with dogs, servants and supplies. In latter years most of the provisions were purchased from the store at Newington. The order was of some magnitude and included: 1 200 lbs sugar, 15 lbs tea, 100 dozen eggs, 4 complete sides of bacon, 30 lbs cheese, 500 lbs bread flour, a 'muid' of potatoes (i.e. three bushel sacks) which had to be augmented by a further 200 lbs half-way through July; 2 cases brandy, 1 case whisky, 2 cases gin and 6 bottles sherry. The store at Newington would also deliver, weekly, a prodigious amount of fresh vegetables from the middle of June to the end of the first week in August.

The hazards of road travelling in those days were experienced by everyone, but Wac found he had additional problems. There was an Afrikaans landowner, a near neighbour of Wac's, through whose property Wac had to travel when he visited his farm Ravenscourt (which he inherited on the death of his father-in-law). On a drift through which the road went, this farmer had constructed a 'corduroy' – a series of poles or logs bound together to make a substitute bridge. The Afrikaner disliked the annual invasion of 'rooinecks' to his part of the world, and particularly disliked Wac who he considered to be the arch 'jingo'. So the old man sabotaged his corduroy by removing some of the logs. Each time Wac passed that way his vehicle became hopelessly stuck in the mud.

Wac was regarded by his neighbours in the lowveld as something of a 'Makhulu-baas' – a 'Big White Chief'. The young Unger girls, who camped under canvas on Sparta and always went on foot through the bush, armed with a gun which was used only if they were in danger, watched with some awe as Wac's vehicles rumbled by, loaded with khaki-clad huntsmen bristling with guns. One of the Unger girls remembers feeling 'somewhat inferior' because at Campbell's camp china crockery was used, whereas at Sparta theirs was only tin! But each to his own. Fun and happiness was had at all the camps, and all have stories to tell of the good old days. One of the funniest and oft-told tales to come out of Sparta occurred in the very early days, when the first Mrs Varty shooed away what she assumed to be her husband's golden

107

labrador with a kitchen towel, only to discover that the dog had been tied up at the time, and it had been a lion who had turned tail and fled before the mistress of the camp! (This story is a little similar to a tale concerning MalaMala's owner of a much more recent vintage. At the camp the manager was having a great deal of trouble with a troop of baboons who insisted on making continuous merry in the jakalsbessie tree which overhangs the boma. Every method imaginable was tried to dislodge the primates, who posed a messy if not serious threat to the guests dining below them. When firing into the tree failed to disperse the animals, the manager informed the owner, Mike Rattray, of the impasse. The 'boss' stood underneath the tree and yelled '*voetsek*' – which is the South African way of saying 'get the hell out' – and the baboons, with tails between their legs, slunk back into the bush never to return.)

Wac's guests knew him as a warm, genial and generous man – the 'perfect host'. One old lady, the widow of a guest who hunted at MalaMala in the thirties, recalls how Wac made everyone, from humble employee at the sugar-mill to the Prime Minister, feel at home. Each year, the old lady recounts, as she and her husband first spied the bougainvillea at the entrance of the camp, her 'heart would turn over'.

From the first, Wac had provided specimens of birds and game for museums both in South Africa and abroad. Kudu, reedbuck, jackal, baboon, porcupine, squirrel, Roan antelope, sassaby and a rare hyena Bruyère, were some of the animals which were carefully skinned and despatched to grateful recipients. Live specimens were sent off too – the Johannesburg zoo was pleased to receive a Wild dog. Officials from museums and zoos all over the world knew they would be welcome at MalaMala, so that apart from the usual peppering of celebrities around the camp fire, there were also always people of interest.

The shooting of specimens had to be halted in 1938 due to an outbreak of foot-and-mouth disease in the lowveld. The outbreak necessitated the destruction of all domestic stock in the area, which meant that all the cattle belonging to the resident blacks had to be slaughtered. The unfortunate beasts were assembled on the farm Toulon

and shot. The graves of the hundreds of beasts – huge long grassy mounds – can still be seen on the right-hand side of the road from Skukuza airport to MalaMala.

In Europe war clouds were beginning to gather, clouds which would cast their shadow even on the far-distant wilderness in the South African lowveld. In 1939 the last official MalaMala camp was held for the duration of the war. While at MalaMala in 1941 Wac heard the sad news of his wife's death after a short illness which had started while she was visiting the camp at the beginning of July. In 1944 Wac's eldest son, Athol, for whom he had held such high hopes, was lost over North Africa. One of Wac's dearest pals, a member of that first hunting party – Dymock Crofts – was also killed in active service. There were others of the 'old guard' who would not be returning from the front.

Once the TCL had given up ranching in the block, (they had sold

A crocodile on its
way from Malamala
to the Durban Museum.
(Hamish Campbell)

their property, Toulon, in 1934) the private landowners realized the
need for some co-operative scheme whereby their farms could be
protected from poachers, and supervised by a white ranger. A solution
was provided by an organization called the Transvaal Land Owners
Association, who took over the administration of what was then called
the Sabi Private Game Scheme. The subscribing members paid for a
white ranger who lived at Toulon, and who was responsible for making
the necessary payments to the various black staff on the farm, as well as
keeping an eye on the farms themselves. (This arrangement continued
until 1950 when a new association was formed, called the Sabi Sand
Wildtuin, of which Wac was the first president).

110

By 1941 there were twenty-five farms in the block comprising 80 000 morgen. 1 000 black men, women and children were staying on the farms, either as squatters or as a source of labour for the absentee landowners. In that year the ranger employed by the TLOA (Transvaal Land Owners Association), was Leo Lownds, who left at the beginning of 1941 to serve in the Forces. The position he rather suddenly vacated was thrust upon his wife Esmé who became the first, and perhaps the only, woman game ranger of such a large tract of land, in the world. This intrepid woman lived alone in the ranger's house at Toulon. Some army chaps taught her how to use a firearm (which Harry Kirkman loaned her) and, with only a smattering of the local lingo, she set about in a most determined manner administering the 'block'. Esmé, now a sprightly eighty-seven year old, recalls that she was rarely bothered by lions (although she always felt a little apprehensive travelling alone in her truck at night), but she was more afraid of snakes which took to inhabiting the roof of her house and entering her home by slithering under the back or front doors. Esmé constructed a concrete barricade which fitted snugly against each door. While these prevented snakes from crossing her threshold, guests were obliged to step high when entering her home.

Esmé came to rely almost entirely on two black men: Pete (who was the ranger at Toulon) and Shoes, who had once been a police 'boy' and fortunately could speak English. They helped her learn the roads and deal with all eventualities on the sixteen farms and nine camps, which could mean coping with problems ranging from white ant invasions to poachers. Esmé found it was not easy being a woman, let alone a woman on her own, in the bush; she says she had to bring the black people to accept that once she donned her white coat (which she used as a badge of her station), she was 'no longer a woman, but the *ranger*'. Eventually her judgement was accepted in all things, even in paternity and other family matters, of which she became the unwilling arbiter. She explains that she found it essential to swear: 'men listen to you better if you swear' she declares. Once it was reported to her that two lions had been fighting; together with Shoes (the latter armed with only an assegaai) she went to investigate, in case one of the lions should have been badly wounded. They didn't find a wounded lion, but Esmé still has the photograph of the tree up which one lion had fled. The clawmarks of the other lion in the soft bark of the tree are clearly visible at least fifteen feet from the ground. Shoes was an experienced 'lion man'. He had saved Leo Lownds' life by shooting a lion in the head while it crouched on top of his master. Shoes now served Leo's wife as faithfully.

Esmé remembers how she loved going to MalaMala, for, as she explains things there 'went like clockwork'. Well-trained servants waited at the little tables in the boma, and the food was superb. Even in the war years, there were always interesting people at the winter camps, and Esmé thoroughly enjoyed the unaccustomed company.

For at least nine months of the year she was the only white woman in the block, in fact she and Monty, the manager of the store at Newington, were the only white people in the entire area (discounting of course those in the Kruger Park over in the east). Sometime in the forties Esmé found herself involved in a macabre event which occurred at Newington. Monty had formed an alliance with a beautiful black girl called Shonasaan, which apart from being against the law at the time, was also against the wishes of the girl's former black lover. Shonasaan demanded to be allowed to go back to her lover. Monty confided in Esmé, who tried to persuade him to let the girl go before there was trouble. Monty vowed that he would rather die, as he could not live without Shonasaan. The latter must somehow have got word to the police that she was being kept at the house behind the store against her will, for they came one night to release her. Monty refused to open the door. Two shots were heard. Monty had first shot his Shonasaan and then put the gun to his own head. He died on the way to hospital. Esmé felt the loss of her only friend and neighbour keenly. The closing chapter of her life in the bushveld was also not a happy one. Leo came back from the war ill with tuberculosis, and so, sadly, they had to leave the bushveld which she had grown to love so well.

In 1946 regular camps at MalaMala were resumed, and that year and

Wac with King George VI,
Princess Margaret and
Princess Elizabeth (back
to camera); at a
gathering before the
Royal visit to the
Kruger National Park.
1947.
(Hamish Campbell)

the next, because of drought conditions, game arrived in enormous numbers from the Kruger Park, to drink at the Sand river. It was estimated that these large herds, particularly of wildebeest, destroyed at least two hundred acres of grass by trampling it down in their haste to get to the water.

'This was a very happy camp after the terrible war years' wrote Alec Logan in the camp journal of 1946: 'Just like old times. We all put on weight thanks to the wonderful table provided by our Good Host'. During July Logan placed a kill on the sand beside the river in front of the camp, so that the guests could witness the vultures operating. It took just ten minutes for the first bird to find the carcass, and in an hour hundreds of birds were there. Within two hours there was nothing left of the carcass but bones.

A sad little party erected a bronze plaque, to the memory of their friend Dymock Crofts, on the giant rocks at the foot of Sithlawayise hill. Later other plaques would be fastened there…

In 1947 the British Royal Family visited South Africa, and included in their tour a spell at the Kruger National Park. Wac was asked to

Len Grice with tracker
"Matches", and the
leopard he shot north
of Campbell koppies.
1948

(Len Grice)

accompany the Royal party through the Park as a game spotter. Plans
were made for the King and Princess Elizabeth to go to MalaMala to
shoot lion, but these unfortunately had to be scrapped at the last minute
because of a shortage of time.

Despite the drought, the grass had recovered by 1948, but because
there were plentiful water sources, and the game was scattered, lion
were hard to find. That year at the camp, Wac's guests presented him
with a surprise birthday present – a new lighting plant for the camp.
Wac was delighted.

There is an amusing footnote to the camp report of that year. Alec
Logan's wife was invited as a guest for the first time, and she had
threatened to supervise the kitchen. Logan added that his wife was
welcome to go into the kitchen, provided that she didn't 'alter the style

of our MalaMala *soup*'! There was something very special about this soup, as the following verse, penned by 'one who was there' indicates:

I have heard it said that MalaMala soup
Will cure anything from tapeworm to croup.
Rich and wholesome it stands on its own,
As the finest 'muti' I have ever known
The cook would not tell me what goes into the pot,
But from what I could gather, it's a hell of a lot.
Nothing is wasted and nothing is spurned,
It all goes in to be steadily churned,
And served piping hot with the evening dinner
You abandon all hope of getting thinner.
For having once eaten it, I know for sure,
Like Oliver Twist you will ask for some more!

By 1950 guests were being requested not to shoot female or young lions as, due to trapping on the farm Gowrie, north of MalaMala where cattle ranching was taking place, the lion population was decreasing. Other game was, however, still being seen in large numbers. Sable antelope came in great troops from the west to drink at the river, lying up on an area south of the camp every afternoon, and at the river on the MalaMala-Flockfield boundary, game came in hundreds to drink. For that reason, the road beside the river which became a busy thoroughfare with migrating game, was called 'West Street', after the main road in the city of Durban. This great migration of game from the Kruger Park took place each winter until the veterinary fence was constructed. Strangely enough, one animal which was being seen so seldom that it was feared the species was becoming extinct was the warthog.

The camp of winter 1951 belonged to Old Two-toes. For two years the spoor of a lion with two toes missing had been observed. Although some hunters had glimpsed the lion, he had proved too cunning to fall prey to a hunter's bullet. Alec Logan was determined to get him. He had had to put an injured zebra out of its misery, so decided to use the

115

carcass as bait, placing it beside a waterhole on the Matshaphiri stream where Old Two-toes spoor was seen. On visiting the site the following morning Logan found that the lion had had a feed and a drink, and had dragged the zebra carcass under a bank, concealing the red meat by pulling loose skin over it. Logan knew that the lion was not only extremely artful, but was intending to return. Logan himself returned early in the afternoon, when all sensible lions would be taking their afternoon naps. He and his tracker, Zaba, crept silently through the bush, following the lion's spoor; cutting each twig before it would snag on Logan's khaki trousers and make a noise, they went as Logan described it 'at half a snail's pace... like ghosts'. There, across a donga, not thirty feet away from them lay the old lion, fast asleep. One shot from the .375 Holland & Holland Magnum, and the old beast died without a groan. What a tale of trial and tribulation his old body had to tell. His magnificent black-maned head and shoulders emerged from a body hairless and emaciated, badly scarred from a trap which the lion at one time must have dragged with him. He had only a stump of a tail, half a back foot was missing, and his teeth were badly smashed. Two old .303 bullets were removed from his body. Mercifully an end was put to the life of Old Two-toes. Logan wrote that the Shangaans were so delighted that he had removed this potential man-eater from the camp surrounds that for the first and only time the local blacks ran forward to greet him as he returned from the hunt, and took his hand in both of theirs, a custom denoting thanks and gratitude of a high order.

In October 1951 Wac made his farm MalaMala over into the ownership of his only surviving son, Urban, apparently to avoid death duties. In December of that year the new owner, accompanied by Len Grice, Jimmy Whittle and Mike Harvey went to the bushveld for an unaccustomed summer visit. The heat was excessive, the temperature reaching 105° in the shade. Large amounts of liquid were consumed. The purpose of the trip was to study the habits of lions, and make an estimation of their numbers. As a result of this investigation, Urban decided that in order to encourage the increase of resident lion populations, the whole of MalaMala was to be closed to motor traffic.

116

Wac and Colonel
Stevenson-Hamilton

Hunting should henceforth be carried out only on foot or on horseback; no cars were to leave camp before sunrise; no shooting from trees or over bait would be allowed, and no lionesses or young lions were to be shot. He recommended that the noisy lighting plant (was this the birthday gift?) should be replaced by a battery plant.

And so changes were coming about as the old order gave way to the new.

The following year Urban built a landing strip next to the river in front of the camp, so that he would not have to cross a sometimes swollen river in the summer months, coming from his old landing strip of Eyrefield. He also ploughed a hundred acres of land south of the camp, where he planted chillies. This enterprise was soon discontinued due to the interest the game took in the new vegetation.

While Urban wrote reports on his frequent, sometimes monthly, visits to MalaMala during the summer months, his father continued to present the annual winter game report which was sent to the Provincial Secretary of the Transvaal, and later to the newly-appointed Director of Fauna and Flora. No longer, however, could Wac preface the reports, as

117

Wac and Eric Louw
July 1953
(Dennis Cleaver)

formerly, with the words 'my farms'. It could not have been easy for him.

The first elephants were seen on MalaMala, near Buffalo bush, in February 1953. There was a good crop of marula fruit on the trees that year, which perhaps enticed them to that area. Urban and his American wife Toni stayed for a large part of the year in camp, living in a house which they had built south of the rondavels. In the autumn of that year Alec Logan, camp 'commandant' since the first MalaMala camp, and Wac's dearest friend and hunting companion, died of cancer. Urban wrote in his journal: 'No finer sportsman ever lived. Those of us who knew him will always remember him with a rifle slung on his shoulder

118

standing with his thumbs tucked into his belt… His spirit will forever haunt MalaMala and he will be with us around the camp fire.' Wac was devastated by the loss of his friend. Urban said his father was now 'like a ship without a rudder'. Yet another brass plaque was sadly fastened to the giant rock at Sithlawayise hill. On the plaque was enscribed: 'In cherished memory of a great sportsman and lovable character FA Logan – "Alec". Died October 11th 1953. He will ever be remembered by his lifelong pals especially Wac and all those who were privileged to meet him over 25 years of happy association at MalaMala'.

Dick Kinsman took over the running of the camp, followed by Len Grice, and the flow of guests still continued in the winter months. Wac himself, still a steady shot, accounted for lion and cheetah. On the surface it seemed that things were going on as before. The new Director of the Durban museum, Dr PA Clancey, went up annually now, in the

Bertie Blevins, Wac, Jackson and Dick Kinsman. 1954
(Mrs Kinsman)

place of Taffy Boyce to collect specimens of birds for his museum. Many of the displays of birds in their natural habitats, which can be seen in the museum today, were painstakingly collected and arranged from material gleaned at MalaMala. Interesting observations concerning the game were still meticulously recorded by Wac. He noted that a honeybadger had killed three full-grown wildebeest bulls by first emasculating them. He also watched a fight between a tree leguaan and a mongoose. The leguaan had the mongoose by the nape of the neck, and only let go when Wac's tracker, Zaba, frightened it away. The third incident, about which a poem was written, concerned a zebra and one of the guests, Mr Eric Louw, who was the Minister of Foreign Affairs in the Government at the time. A zebra was seen lying motionless on the ground. As it was assumed that the animal was dead, Wac drove his jeep to within ten yards of the beast, which still didn't stir. Zaba then approached it on foot. When the tracker was almost on top of the zebra it raised its head slowly and got to its feet – looked at the open-mouthed guests in the jeep and made off. Eric Louw composed the following verse:

The Sleeping Zebra

A zebra asleep,
Ten yards from a jeep!
Please don't make us weep
With a story so steep!

There was laughter and jesting
Despite Campell's protesting
And three natives attesting
That the zebra was nesting,
Or perchance, even resting,
Ten yards from the jeep.

There was scoffing and jeering,

By all within hearing
Whilst Louw was declaring
With vigour and heat,
His face like a beet,
'I saw it asleep
Ten yards from the jeep'.

This vote of no confidence,
In men of such prominence,
Sobri-e-ty and competence,
Was a shock and a blow,
To Baas Campbell and Louw.

Wac was not above having some sport at the expense of his guests. One of his party had a recording of lions roaring. Wac had him play this at sundown as the guests were having their drinks under the jakalsbessie tree in front of what is now the dining room. The result was absolute chaos. The kitchen staff locked themselves in the kitchen; some of the servants climbed the nearest tree; guests flew to their rooms, some appearing with rifles, and running in all directions. 'You can image their remarks' wrote Wac in his journal, 'when they found it was only a hoax!' A week later he played the game again on a new batch of guests. This time the servants were 'in' on it and were told to report to Wac that there were lions in the cattle kraal. The result was as hilarious as on the first occasion.

In 1960 Wac submitted his last game report. For more than thirty years he had carefully observed and recorded what had occurred. In that last report he noted that warthog were now fortunately on the increase, while Sable antelope were on the decline. He warned that the veterinary fence which the authorities were in the process of erecting between the Kruger Park and the Sabi Sand Windtuin would prove to be 'a nightmare in upkeep... and a farce and a lovely arrangement for the lions to catch the game'.

He mentioned at the end of his report that 130 guests had enjoyed

"Mine Host". Wac, July 1954

(Dennis Cleaver)

Malamala camp. 1954

The boma. 1953

123

Dr Bodenstein weighing
his lion on the old
Salter scale

(Mrs Bodenstein)

Children being forced to 'absorb' the dead lion's magic and strength.
(Dennis Cleaver)

MalaMala that season, more than half of these having been women and children, a new development, surely due to Urban's influence. For the only time in all those years of signing official game reports, Wac added the word 'Colonel' under his signature. He never went back to MalaMala.

Two years later, on the 17 September having been confined for a great deal of the time to a wheel chair, Wac died at Muckleneuk (the gracious home on the Durban Berea which his parents had built at the beginning of the century, and which after his wife's death Wac had shared with his sister Killie) a lonely and frequently cantankerous old man of eighty-two years. He was given a large and colourful funeral at Verulam, a

Wac, the patriarch, reading letters from home for members of his staff.

town just north of Mount Edgecombe, and buried in the cemetery where members of his own and the Armstrong family had been laid to rest before him. Hundreds of Zulus, mostly in full regalia, came to pay their last respect to 'Ntaba-kayi-konjwa' – 'the mountain which is *not* pointed at'. Wac had seven years previously given his home Muckleneuk to the City of Durban to be used as a museum; now his generosity reached beyond his death; he had willed the corneas of his eyes to the Bantu Blind Society. Two young Zulu men regained their sight thanks to the thoughtfulness of Mfo-ka-Mashu – the son of Marshall.

126

Urban continued to visit MalaMala. He built more accommodation, including the building which now forms the lounge and diningroom. Through a travel company he began marketing MalaMala as a bushveld paradise where the camera replaced the gun. He and his wife, with the aid of a ranger, ran it until he sold it in 1964 to MalaMala Ranch (Pty) Ltd, a company managed by Loring Rattray, who was also a sugar farmer from Natal. Rattray already owned Exeter and Wallingford in the Sabi Sand Wildtuin; now the prize of them all was his.

After forty years when MalaMala had become a byword with famous as well as simple folk, as a huntsman's paradise, it was entering a period of game-viewing and tourism on a scale unique in South Africa. The Rattray years were beginning.

Ceratotheca triloba.
Wild foxglove

SUMMER

'... Sweet as summer.'
Shakespeare, *Henry VIII*

Summer in the bushveld is the wet season. The average rainfall of between 400 and 600 millimetres usually falls between October and March.

From the air the scene is very different from the departure from the highveld on a cold crisp winter morning. Now Red bishop birds cling to the tall grass at the side of the run-way at Jan Smuts airport, while the Wild foxgloves (Ceratotheca triloba) flower pink beside the tarmac at Skukuza. Previously dry watercourses run now with water; from the air the flow of the Sand river looks full and brown.

The genial Kirk drives us along the Skukuza road; to either side of us all is green and lush. The trees are in full leaf and the grass looks rich and full-bodied. There is the usual exitement at seeing the first game: baboon, impala and zebra. The impala have young at their sides: long-legged, as yet without the distinctive black socks which their parents wear, they romp among the herds of females, moving with short jumpy movements. Kirk stops the bus while we admire a mother warthog and her four babies. The piglets follow in a line; when mama halts so do they, and stare at us with little grey noses in the air. As our driver changes into first gear, the noise sends the little family trotting off into the bush, tails erect.

Pink Wild gladiolus dot the open areas, and blue Commelina modesta sprawls over the short grass.

Although it is hot, our huts in the camp are cool, as is the dining-room, from where we watch the weavers and the starlings having their

128

Commelina modesta

Gladiolus brachyphyllus. This species is rarely collected as it flowers for only a short period. From bloom to seed takes approximately three weeks. No illustration appears in any reference book.

129

THE SHANGAAN LION SONG
(with thanks to Thayi Mhlamba)

Yimpi ya hlula wezize,
Sibabona ba phike kani.
Wa hlula we zizwe.

Who wins the fight?
We have seen them lying.
We win; we win.

(Translation by Norman Mabunda,
Malamala)

Fragrant herb
growing in sandy
soil on the river-
bank

Cucumis sp.

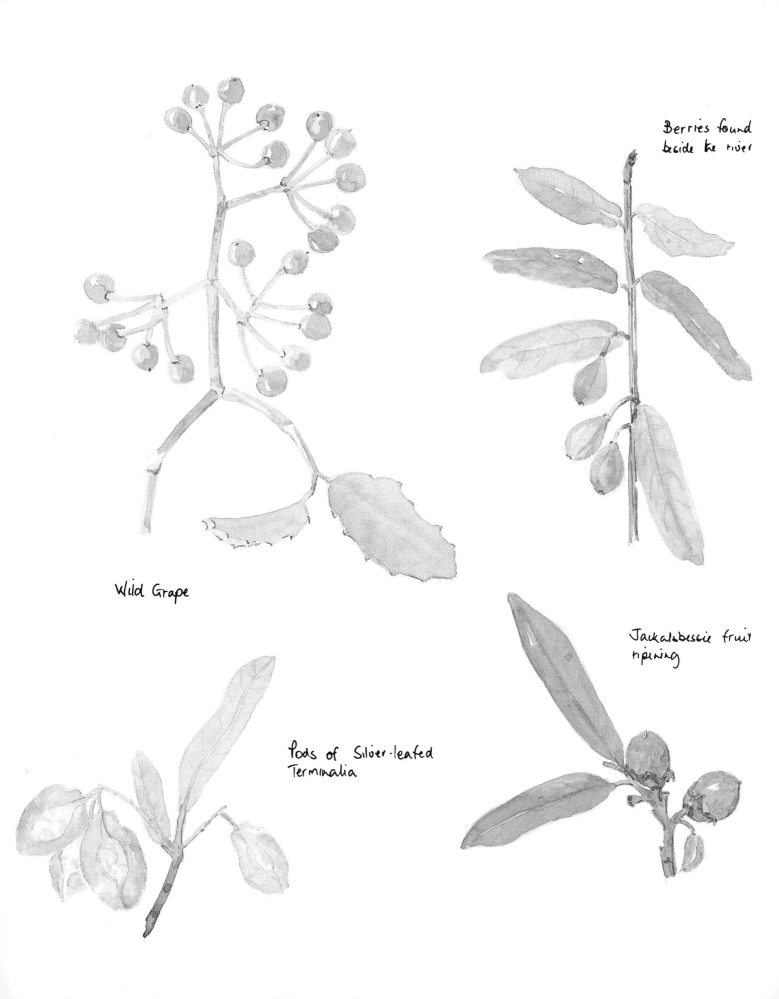

Berries found
beside the river

Wild Grape

Jackalsbessie fruit
ripening

Pods of Silver-leafed
Terminalia

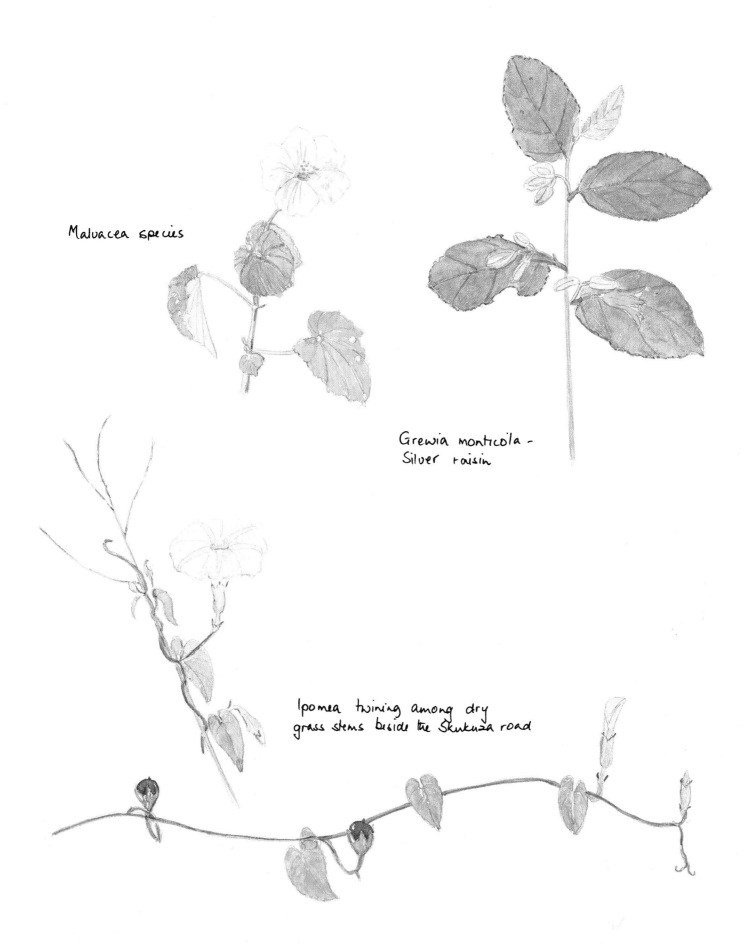

Malvacea species

Grewia monticola -
Silver raisin

Ipomea twining among dry
grass stems beside the Skukuza road

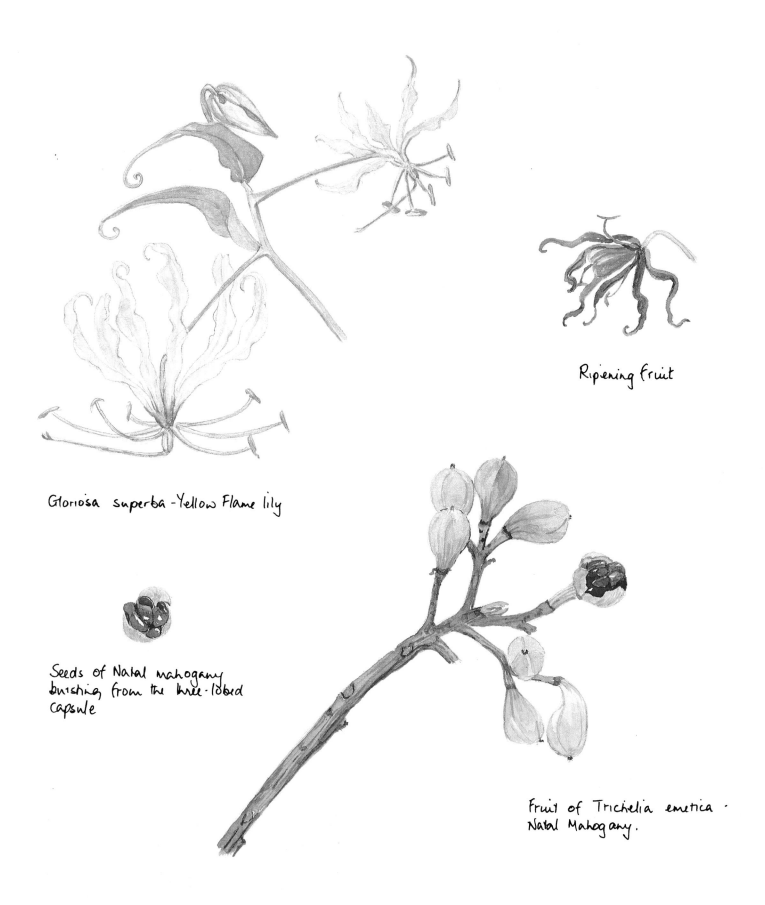

Ripening fruit

Gloriosa superba - Yellow Flame lily

Seeds of Natal mahogany
bursting from the three-lobed
capsule

Fruit of Trichelia emetica -
Natal Mahogany.

midday crumbs outside the window. There are great dark pools of shadow under the huge ebony trees, and across the river everything is still and peaceful in the noonday heat.

After lunch I sit under a giant intombi tree in the camp and talk to old Tayi Mhlaba, who was once one of Wac Campbell's trackers. Tayi is an old man now, he does not know how old, but events which he remembers makes me believe he is well into his eighties. He has come from the Gazankulu homeland to talk to me about the old times. I have an interpreter – a young black man employed at the camp who is, I can see, both elated by this important task assigned to him, and in awe of the legendary figure whose stories he will be privileged to hear. Although the shade is deep under our tree, the old man declines to discard any of his warm clothing. He wears a turtle-necked fairisle sweater and a jacket. On his lap he clutches a parcel wrapped in a cloth. He unwraps the parcel and proudly shows me two framed photographs. One is a full-length picture of a young black man standing beside a slain lion: Tayi in the mid-thirties with the beast which, he tells us, he shot in the mouth. The other photograph, taken on the farm Exeter, is of a very young Mike Rattray, who poses beside the first lion that he ever shot. (An amusing incident concerns this very photograph: old Tayi was invited by Mike and Norma Rattray to the opening of Kirkman's Kamp in 1983. Tayi pitched up there too with his precious parcel. It took some persuading on Mike Rattray's part to prevent the old man from flaunting this record of lion killing at the party which was bristling with conservationists.)

I show Tayi the photograph I have of him, taken by Len Grice in 1935; a young man, garbed in a sarong-like skirt, solemnly facing the camera, little knowing that fifty years hence his likeness will appear in a book.

Tayi shows us where the original huts were built in Campbell's time, and takes us to the tree from which, in the old days, the Salter scale hung, on which the trophies were weighed. He tells us how the black women brought their children to stand on the dead lions, so that some of the beasts' strength would pass into their little bodies. He chuckles as

134

Kudu bull -leaping away through the bush

New-winged beetle
Family: Lycidae.
Aptly called the
"Pumpkin" beetle.
Found at camp.

Lion's Eye -
Tricliceras longepedunculata.
Flat with faces close up in
the mid afternoon.

he remembers how some unwilling little legs
had to be forced straight, so that the toes could
be made to touch the lion's skin.

Tayi has a funeral which he must attend, so having
partaken of a good meal, and greeted many old friends
in the camp, he is transported back to his home about thirty
miles away, where he will no doubt return to sitting in the
sun outside his hut, dreaming of the days that used to be.

It is still hot after tea when we leave for our game drive,
but we are all nevertheless armed with sweaters and jackets
as the air can get cold when the sun sets. There is a heavy bank
of cloud in the south-west, which, we are told, may bring rain later.

We head towards the river. The veld is full of flowers: little orange
Lion's eye (Tricliceras longepedunculata), their flat faces open to the
sun; blue and yellow Commelina, purple Turbina, and nearer the river
pink Devil's thorn (Dicerocaryum zanguebarium). The river reeds are in
full leaf, and beneath the sharp leaves of the Wild date palm (Phoenix
reclinata), the wiry orange stems which in the spring bore tiny yellow
flowers, now support rows of shiny green dates which will later ripen to
yellow. A liquor is made from the sap of this palm by the black people,
while the 'heart' is used as a vegetable. The leaves are used in hat and
basket making – altogether a most useful plant. There are hippo tracks
in the river sand, where some lone beast has come to sample the lush
grass which grows on the bank. The river flows strongly and muddily; a
pair of European swallows sit on the boom beside the bridge, while

Ripe fruit of
the Date palm.

Swallows sitting near the bridge over the river
Left: wire-tailed swallow, a resident;
Right: European swallow, a summer visitor.

Colotis vesta ♂
Veined Orange

Grewia species

Wild Jasmine

136

Cassia abbreviata

Emperor dragonfly -
Anax imperator.

Thistle sp. growing
on river bank

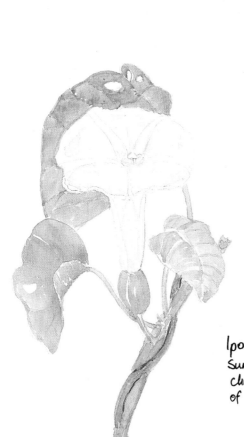

Ipomea albivenia - Wild Cotton. Flowers open from
sunset to noon the following day. I found this one
climbing over a magic guarri bush just south
of Paraffin Drift.

Swallows in flight
Left: European; right: wire-tailed.

several Wire-tailed swallows, orange caps shining in the sun, dip and turn after the insects which rise up from the cooling earth. A solitary Common sandpiper walks at the water's edge. A Red-backed shrike flies across our path, a newly-returned migrant; another traveller has returned, the ubiquitous Woodland kingfisher whose musical trill is a joyous characteristic of the bushveld in summer.

At Piccadilly pans, the giant plumes of the Scilla nervosa have lost their petals, but still stand erect in the long grass. A pair of Wahlberg's eagles perch in a dead leadwood tree. In the fork of another leadwood tree, a Leopard orchid (Ansellia gigantea) is flowering, its yellow blossoms shining against the grey of the bark, its wiry roots taking life from the air.

On the river road we come across a pair of baggy-trousered elephants having their evening meal of supple Taxacantha vines. Our presence does not disturb them, in fact the elephant nearest us is so relaxed that he crosses one back foot over the other leg, rather as if he were waiting for a bus! Beyond him a flock of tiny Blue waxbills flit into the thick bush: we hear their sweet 'weety-weet' call above the munching of the elephants. Diederik and Red-chested cuckoos call – the latter will no doubt continue calling 'Piet-my-vrou' into the long hours of the night.

We stop to watch a pair of Fork-tailed drongos harassing a Tawny eagle. The eagle, who no doubt poses a threat to the drongos' nestlings, refuses to budge from his perch on the tree; he merely winces and ducks his head as the drongos in turn fly in and aim vicious pecks at the eagle's head.

Further along the road we come across another battle. Two male giraffe stand beside one another, legs firmly on the ground, and in turn

Woodland kingfisher.
Arrives at Mala Mala in November,
staying til April or May.

Flowers of Leopard orchid –
Ansellia gigantea

swing at each other with their long muscular necks. Each blow echoes with a resounding thud. While we watch neither is able to deal a telling blow with his horns, only the sides of the heads and the necks make contact. The sparring ceases although there appears to be no obvious victor.

Hostility seems to be in the air of this hot summer afternoon, for soon after the giraffe encounter, we see two impala rams crossing swords (horns) with each other. Heads almost touching the ground, horns interlocked, one gladiator forces the other to back-track, surely a demonstration of victory.

Yellow spikes of the Marama bean flowers (Tylosema fassoglense) still show above the short grass near Campbell's koppies and further north west tiny white flowers and pale pink Vigna vexillata grow. In an area where the Strychnos (Monkey apple) bushes are still bare and black after the winter burning, a pair of White rhino stare at us from a distance, then turn sideways and move off; the bush is too thick for us to follow.

Our disappointment turns to delight a few minutes later when our ranger spots a leopard only a few metres off the road. This time the bush doesn't stop us, and we follow the huge male cat doggedly as he strides through the veld. Every now and then he pauses to sniff the grass. His supple, plush pelt is a burnished gold in the light of the setting sun. Suddenly the leopard appears very agitated: he breaks into a trot and rushes to and fro, apparently on the track of something. He makes off

Male leopard on the hunt

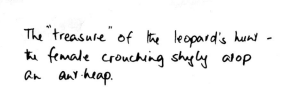

The "treasure" of the leopard's hunt - the female crouching shyly atop an ant-heap.

Colias electo electo -
Clouded Yellow ♂

Colotis danae ♂
Scarlet Tip
Common in summer

Cynthia cardui ♂
Painted Lady

Papilio morania
White Lady swallowtail

Catopsella florella ♀
African Migrant - Yellow form.

Colotis calais ♀ —
Topaz Arab

Acraea terpsicore neobule ♂
Wandering Donkey

Colotis ione ione ♂
Purple Tip.
Wet season form

Pinacopteryx eriphia ♂
Zebra White.

Charaxes achaemenes ♀
Bush charaxes

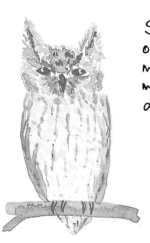

hurriedly with a change of direction, and we see ten metres away, the treasure of his hunt, a tawny female leopard, paler and smaller than the male, sitting atop an antheap. She coyly jumps from her perch and runs deeper into the bush. The leopard follows. Our ranger explains that normally the female would approach the male, but the vehicles which surround the pair (some now shining their spotlights) are inhibiting the shy female. Although we are tempted to continue following the pair we leave the male to his overtures, hoping that his endeavours will have a happy ending.

The sun slipped below the horizon while we were engrossed with our leopards. We drive to a wide open area on Eyrefield where Urban Campbell once had his airstrip. The short grass is a mass of lily plants; where in spring the pink Crinium buphanoides flowered, now only the strap-like plaited leaves of the grey-green plants remain. There is a loud chorus of frogs coming from the pools of water which reflect the last pink tinges of the sunset. A Black-backed jackal slinks off across the veld at our approach. We have our sundowner drinks in this open area, looking over the tops of the distant trees to the dark shadows of the mountain escarpment in the west. The sky is heavy with purple rain-clouds.

A herd of wildebeest, their eyes shining like a cluster of village lights, graze at the fringe of the open area. The spotlight lights up more than a dozen new-born babies – pale little calves, the colour of impala – who mill about among the dark-brown cows.

Further on, on the road which runs past the Matshaphiri dam, we stop to watch a herd of buffalo grazing; immense eerie shadows in the dark night. Something disturbs them and they begin to stampede – thundering across our path in a great black mass, presenting quite a different aspect to the docile-looking animals which we are accustomed to seeing. Harry Kirkman tells a story concerning one of his trackers who, out following a wounded buffalo, was suddenly charged by the beast who had been hiding in some reeds. The tracker pulled out his knife and stood his ground until the buffalo was almost upon him – then dived sideways at the last minute as the animal thundered past. Seeing

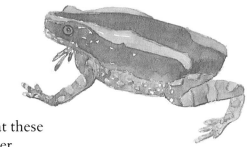

Banded Rubber frog -
Phrynomerus bifasciatus.
His voice like a bird's trill —
heard as the New Pan at night.

the buffalo charging across our path makes it easy to believe that these animals are responsible for more deaths of hunters than any other animal.

We head towards Marthly, where lions were seen at a kill yesterday. On a clearing beside the river we see on the opposite bank, the tawny forms of two lions who are lying beside the half-eaten carcass of a young giraffe. Surrounded by the curtain of darkness, the two lions are like players taking the spotlight on a stage. They perform beautifully for us; occasionally the younger male, cat-like, rubs his tawny-maned head against that of his black-maned companion. Every now and then one or other of them rises, stretches and then flops down in a different position to gnaw half-heartedly on the giraffe carcass. They both look relaxed and replete and very pleased with themselves.

There is a rustling sound to the left of us. John shines the light on to three hippo grazing on the riverbank. Their massively fat hairless bodies glisten in the light. When hippo emerge from the water after sunset, they mark out a pear-shaped area by means of piles of dung. The narrow end of the territory, where the animals emerge from the river, is defended by the males. We are informed that hippos mate in the water, and the females have a gestation period of approximately eight months, after which the mother-to-be takes herself off into the reeds to give birth to a single calf. The baby is able to swim almost immediately.

We bump across the veld on to the road. A Giant eagle owl looks down at us from the branches of a tall tree. The bird blinks in the glare of the spotlight, dropping heavy pink lids over his large brown eyes.

We feel the warm air cooling as we dip down to cross the dry bed of the Mlowathi stream at Paraffin drift. During the course of one of the early camps in the Campbell days, one of Wac's chums, Willie Wiltshire, was driving through this drift in a car, accompanied by a black tracker. The car ran out of petrol at this very spot. Wiltshire sent his tracker to the camp to fetch a tin of petrol. After some hours the tracker returned with the tin, which to Wiltshire's horror was filled not with petrol but with paraffin.
Hence the name of this drift. What

Giant Eagle owl

Heniocha marnois ♂
Marbled Emperor moth

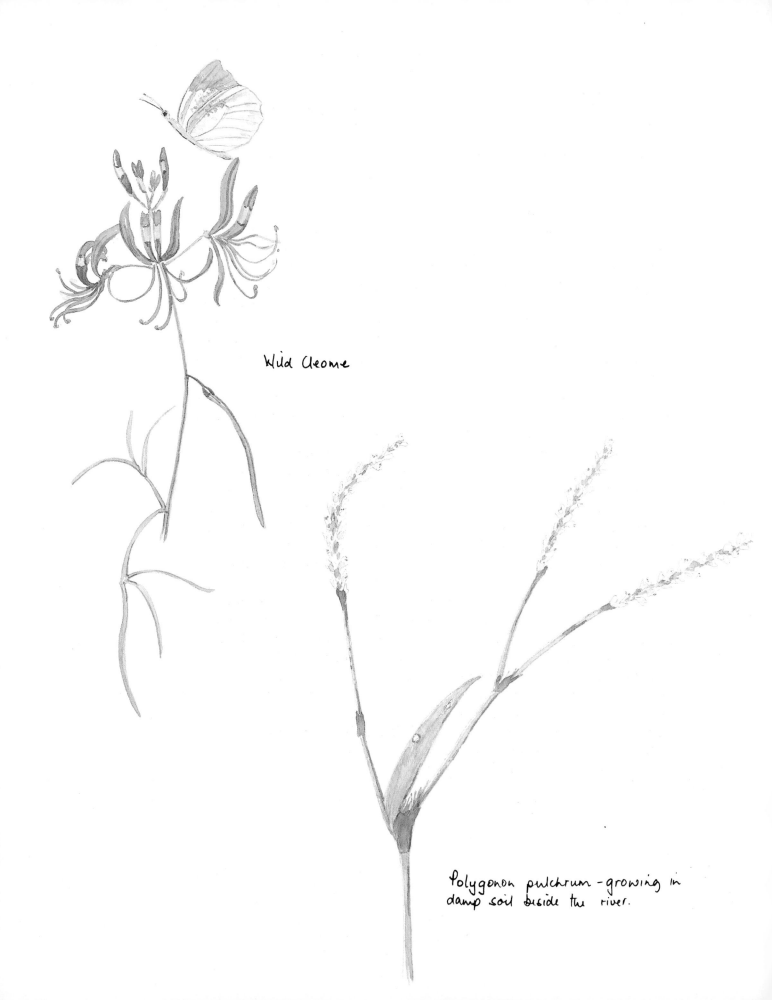

Wild Cleome

Polygonon pulchrum – growing in
damp soil beside the river.

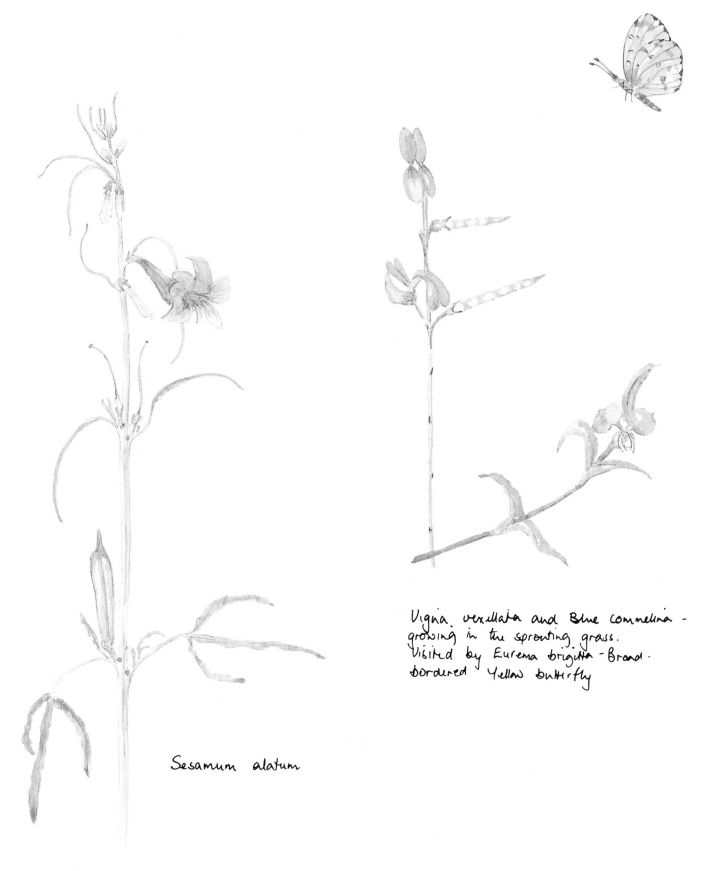

Sesamum alatum

Vigna vexillata and Blue commelina -
growing in the sprouting grass.
Visited by Eurema brigitta - Broad-
bordered Yellow butterfly

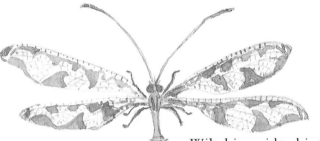

Anaphe reticulata ♀ –
Reticulate Bagnest moth.
The final stage of the
Processionary caterpillars
we saw in June.

Wiltshire said to his tracker is not recorded, (or perhaps the old hunter who told me the story was too polite to say!). Wiltshire, despite having only one eye, had a way with the ladies, and was one of the 'characters' of the early Campbell camps. He was employed as a veterinarian at Natal Estates, and although untrained, performed his duties with skill. Many were the torn limbs of man, horse and dog, which Wiltshire patched up during his years at MalaMala, a rôle subsequently undertaken in the latter years by Len Grice.

As we drive campwards our headlights shine on a Spotted dikkop who stands facing us in the road. The bird has something in its beak. At our approach it spreads its wings in an effort to look menacing; how courageously it stands its ground before the great evil-smelling monster which we must represent. Realizing that we are not going to rob him of his supper, the bird lowers its wings and gets on with the business of devouring its prey – Breviceps frog. The latter has blown itself up in self-defence. In its inflated condition it is too large for the dikkop to swallow. The bird bashes the frog repeatedly on to the road; we hear pitiful squeaks from the frog as it is bounced on the hard road surface. After a few minutes of repeating this procedure, the bird changes its tactics, and laying the frog on the road, pierces it with its sharp beak. There is a loud 'pop'. All that is left of the frog is a pathetic-looking piece of skin, which the bird swallows in one gulp. I am reminded of Eeyore's burst birthday balloon, the present from Piglet in AA Milne's 'Winnie the Pooh'.

We return to camp along the same road we travelled about two hours ago. In that time a spider has woven an intricate cartwheel web, anchored by fine threads which span the road. John shines the light on the large spider who positions herself in the centre of her beautiful trap, waiting for insect prey. We deviate into the bush, so as not to damage this amazing creation – and also, of course, to avoid having the displaced spider land in our laps.

As we near the camp a few drops of rain fall, the start of a lovely soft warm rain which continues to fall through the night. Although the rain necessitates dinner being served in the diningroom, we are compensated

Owl Fly – Ascalaphidae
Seen flying in summer
evenings looking for prey.

Bushveld Rain Frog –
Breviceps adspersus.
Voice : a short chirp
continuously repeated.

146

Moçambique Rain Frog – Breviceps
mossambicus

Waterbuck family

by the pleasure of being able, later, to lie in bed and listen to the sound of the rain dropping softly to the ground from the edge of the thatched roof of our hut.

Our hut faces the river and the east, and through the wide window we can watch the morning sky change from opal to lavender. At first the trees are dark silhouettes, but as the sky lightens they each assume their distinctive forms. Mist rises above the cool water in the river. A family of waterbuck move slowly and gracefully across the flat area between the swimming-pool and the river bank. It was here that small aircraft landed in the old days. How lovely that now such modern intrusions take place out of sight and sound some way away, and nothing disturbs the tranquillity of this little Eden washed clean by the night's rain. Like the first morning.

We drink our coffee on the verandah watched by a cluster of baboons, who sit on the lower branches of a big tree on the river bank, keeping their bottoms off the wet grass, basking in the early morning sun.

We take the Skukuza road for a while (having been formally saluted by the solemn boom-man), and then turn across the airstrip. Crowned plovers, in their schoolboy caps, wheel in the air, uttering their penetrating 'kie-*wiet*'. A Common duiker darts to the left of us, disappearing into the bush. Warthogs kneel as they dig for roots with their hard snouts. A large male lifts his warty face to look at us; a grass root hangs comically over one of his tusks. A cluster of birds sit on the telephone wires overhead. The light from the rising sun catches their wings – like a handful of bright jewels they rise and disperse. These are perhaps the most wonderfully coloured of all bushveld birds – the Carmine bee-eaters. They are among the last of the migrants to return. They breed while wintering north of the equator and must wait until their young are old enough to accompany them on the long journey south.

Male
Scarletchested
sunbird

Carmine Bee-eater –
The jewel of the summer
bird visitors –

Crowned plover –
in schoolboy cap

Cardiospermum species growing on river bank
at Rocky Crossing. Enjoyed by larva of Citrus
Swallowtail butterfly

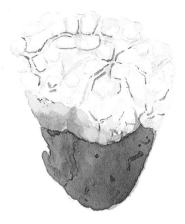

Puff-ball growing in elephant dung at side
of road.

Coprinus micaceus

Maytenus heterophylla - growing in camp

Wild basil

Yellow-billed
Hornbill

Our ranger sees lion spoor in the muddy surface of the road and conveys this information to the other rangers on his radio. Someone else soon picks up more fresh spoor near the Princess Alice bush, tracks which are heading towards the river, so we agree to do the tracking on the far side of the river. For a while it is easy to follow the spoor, with our tracker perched on the bonnet of the vehicle, but after a while the tracks turn into the bush. John and our ranger (the latter armed with a gun) go off together into the bush to investigate.

It is a glorious time for us. We sit in the middle of the dew-sparkling wilderness, with time to admire the filagree patterns of the spiders' webs. We listen to the bush sounds: the faintly hysterical giggling call of the Yellow-billed hornbill, the mournful notes of the Emerald-spotted wood dove; the bright onomatopoeic call of the Black-headed oriole. A pair of Fork-tailed drongos perform some aerobatics in the sky above us, others make their grating noise from trees nearby. A Black cuckoo calls, then a Puffback shrike. Arrow-marked babblers cackle a way off – the bush is alive with the bird symphony.

Our guides return telling us that the lion has changed direction. Our ranger contacts one of his colleagues, who will follow up the spoor: it is an exercise in planning and co-operation. We in the meantime head for an area to the east, where John has spotted vultures circling in the sky. Several of the large birds sit in a dead tree, while others congregate on

Arrow-marked babbler –
one of the noisiest bush birds.

White stork –
Summer migrant
from Europe.

the ground. There are White-backed and bare-necked Lappet-faced vultures in the group. The birds fly off clumsily at our approach. We are disappointed to find that all that remains of a kill is a dark piece of duiker skin, several days old. Our ranger explains that wild creatures cannot afford to pass up any opportunity to obtain food.

We hear on our radio that the lion is walking in our direction, and as we drive along the narrow road, coming towards us is the king of beasts himself. A magnificent black-maned male, he is lord of all he surveys. He is bound on territory-marking, which he does (like any tom-cat worth his salt), by spraying urine on to areas of grass or bush, which will proclaim to any lion intruder that this is his domain, and that trespassers will be prosecuted. Before the lion sprays, he first rubs his head against the tree or bush, in an affectionate sort of way. We follow him through the bush, marvelling at his size and stately bearing, and the wondrous way his huge front paws flap down on to the ground as he walks.

Eurema hecabe
sengalensis ♂
Lowveld Yellow
Found in wet season.
Foodplant: cassia
mimosoides

Around a corner we come across a termitary which is being constructed – the termites are taking advantage of the wet soil to build their new home which may still be standing in hundreds of years' time. This termitary is being constructed in the open, but many are built with trees in their centre – usually a Weeping boer-bean tree (Schotia brachypetala). There is a purpose in this arrangement: the termites benefit from certain minerals which they obtain from the Schotia trees. The termites themselves are responsible for returning nutrients to the

Male Saddlebilled
Stork

Dragonfly. One of the oldest
flying creatures - older by some
150 million years than birds.

Tenebrionid beetle -
"Tok-tokkie". Wingless
beetle which taps its
abdomen on the ground
to attract a mate.

Millipede found near Campbell Koppies. I had drawn
its front and rear when it escaped from its box, never
to be found.

Common Variable Skink - Mabuya varia varia -
found at the camp.

Ground beetle;
Family, Carabidae.
A species which
uses chemicals in
its body as a
defence mechanism.

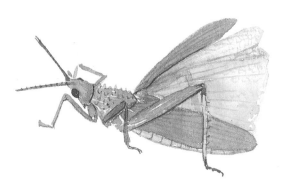

Short-horned grasshopper

Millipede which didn't get away.

Giant land snail. Achatrina
(Drawn life-size) Found on a morning
after rain. It travelled in the back of
the land-rover, leaving a translucent
slimy trail on the plastic seat-cover.

Yellow Pansy —
Junonia hierta cebrene

soil, through the food that they eat. On the large mounded termitaries, which are less pinnacle-like, the grass grows more luxuriantly then elsewhere. This is the reason why the grass covering these 'mounds' is always the first to be grazed.

Other types of ants have been stimulated by last night's rain. Tiny little clay spires appear along the centre of the dirt roads. These were not here yesterday.

Vervet monkeys scamper off as we approach, but can't resist pausing to take a good look at us from the safety of the trees. Last evening the manager of the camp told us that one of his staff had brought him a very new baby monkey, which had fallen from a tree in the camp. The manager wisely decided that the baby should not be kept as a pet. He took the little fellow to where it had been found. He could hear monkey-chatter coming from the other side of a fence. Peering over the fence the manager was confronted by several little black monkey faces looking at him. He held the baby monkey up high, and then placed it on the ground and stood back. In a flash the mother monkey vaulted the fence, snatched up her baby which she appeared to tuck under her arm, and was off to join her troop. A story with a happy ending.

Three stately kudu ewes stand looking in the same direction, the ruffs on their necks stiff and glistening in the sunlight. A while later a male with spiralling horns lifts his nose so that his horns lie across his back as he treads slowly through the thick bush. Blue waxbills flash by, and a White-crowned shrike lands on the branch of an Acacia nilotica tree, whose golden ball flowers look shabby after the night's rain. A pair of Black-crowned tchagra perform their melodious duet.

At Buffalo pans, where the white meringue balls of the Foam Nest frogs hang over the water, a moorhen and a Knob-billed duck float on the brown water.

In the pond where the frog-foam hangs. Moorhen (left); Little Grebe or Dabchick on the right.

We see a Ground hornbill, one of the largest birds in South Africa – glossy black with vivid red patches on eye and throat – carrying a large snake in his curved black beak. The bird lumbers off with flapping wings, and takes off clumsily into some trees and out of sight.

Cerise and yellow lanterns hang from the Large-leafed sickle bushes (Dichrostachys cinerea nyassana); they, too, like the acacia flowers, are bedraggled after the rain. Grazing on the short grass is a lone wildebeest, who, pushed out of the herd, will no doubt soon provide an easy meal for lions. The old fellow lifts his head to look at us, snorts (like a suppressed sneeze), and with a toss of his maned head, canters off.

Our radio comes suddenly alive with an excited voice announcing that cheetah have been found. Explicit directions are given by one of the rangers who has left a branch in the road where the animals moved into the bush. We hurriedly cross back over the river and head south-west. Just where we were directed we find the branch and the tracks of a vehicle leading into thick bush. We all keep our heads well down to avoid overhanging branches. Our ranger switches off the engine and requests the other ranger to 'rev' his vehicle, which will give us a sound bearing. In the sudden silence we hear the sound of the other vehicle's engine, and we turn towards it. In a clearing in the bush are five lithe, magnificent specimens – a mother and four almost adult young. They are perfect examples of nature's ingenuity: long legs, with a small head, and a very slow heart beat, all designed for speed in the chase (these animals can run at a speed of up to seventy-four kilometres per hour for sprints of about two hundred metres); dark spots against a light tawny background make, in daylight, a perfect dappled camouflage. These must be the most elegant creatures of the wild. Dark 'tear-marks' give their faces a sad appearance, but their carriage is proud. The five move, like rippling water, across the bare ground, towards a patch of dry sand where, quite oblivious of our attentions, they sink down gracefully together. They lie, as cats do, partially on their sides, heads upright, legs

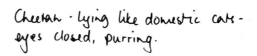

Cheetah - lying like domestic cats - eyes closed, purring.

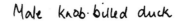

Male knob-billed duck

Cyperus sp.

Single flower of Giant sedge.
Cyperus immensus. The largest
of the sedges at Inabanala. Grows
to a height of two metres

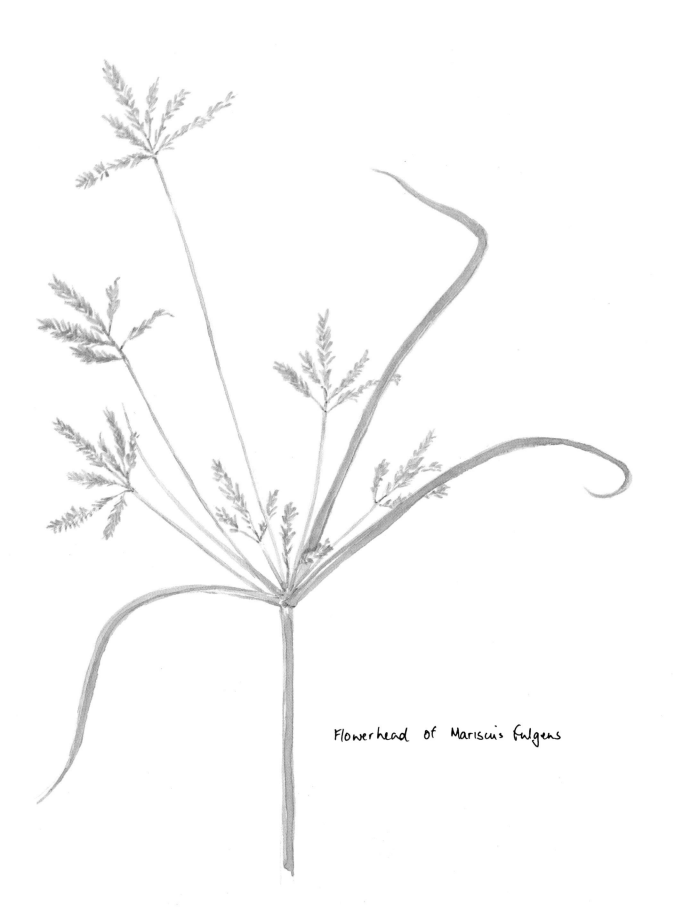

Flowerhead of Mariscus fulgens

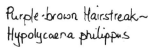
Purple-brown Hairstreak ~
Hypolycaena philippus

Bushman's grape ~
Rhoicissus tridentata.

outstretched, feet intertwined; each animal is touching, even if only slightly, another. Gradually their eyes close and to our utter delight, they begin to purr – a loud rich sound as of a well-oiled tractor engine. There are now three vehicles encircling the cheetah, yet they are unperturbed by our nearness. There is awe on all the faces of the human spectators of this marvellous spectacle. Suddenly the animals are all alert, and sit up with ruffs out, faces all pointing in the same direction. We follow their gaze: a Slender mongoose sits on his haunches, on top of an antheap about fifty metres away, and surveys the predators warily, then slips down and away out of sight. The cheetah sink back on to their sides and begin to purr again.

The sun is high, and although we would stay and watch these beautiful creatures, who soon will begin hunting, the imagined aroma of sizzling bacon calls, and we turn northwards and head for home.

On the road near the turn-off to Flockfield, a male nyala stands in the dappled shade of some trees. A young bull, his lyre-shaped horns are only a foot in length, and more than a dozen white stripes run vertically down his body. With age most of these stripes will disappear. Like the kudu, which he resembles, he has a band across his forehead between his eyes. Soft hair fringes the length of his body; this stands erect when he is roused. Selous, the great hunter of the last century came on a quest to these parts in search of nyala. He eventually found the animal he was seeking, far to the north-east, in an area which is now the northern section of the Kruger National Park.

We are halted by a little group of Dwarf mongooses who romp in the road, some crouch, others sit on their haunches, little teddy-bear noses in the air. Suddenly they are attacked from above by a Dark Chanting goshawk who swoops down on them from a nearby tree.
The tiny creatures scatter and disappear into the
thick grass at the road's edge.
The bird returns to his perch,
and the mongooses
return to the
centre of

Dwarf mongooses

Giant wasp

Natal francolin

the road. Again an attack is launched, again unsuccessful. A strange
performance, as the mongooses look an easy target. After the second
attempt, the bird changes direction, and dives instead into a bush to the
left of the road. Out of the bush, with a great cackling din and a
scattering of feathers, a Natal francolin bursts like a fire-craker. But the
goshawk has missed again, and retires to his tree without his breakfast.
Wanting ours, we hurry on eagerly to camp.

Waterbuck

THE RATTRAY YEARS

Apart from their love of wild life, Wac Campbell and MalaMala's new owner, Loring Rattray, had much in common. Both came from early settler stock; in both there was a Scottish connection; the forebears of both men were Natal pioneers whose industry and foresight were to bring benefits not only to their progeny, but to the country of their adoption.

William Clark, Loring's grandfather on his mother's side, emigrated from Yorkshire with his family, arriving in Durban in 1850. In 1857, then a young man of twenty-three, William bought a property in Pine Street where he started a foundry and wagon-building business. Two years later he married Sarah Jee, who had also emigrated from England, in 1850 with her family. Twenty years later the couple and their four daughters moved to a small-holding to the west of Durban, which Clark bought from the estate of Christopher Joseph Cato. At Camphill – so called because the 45th Regiment (Sherwood Forresters) had camped on this high ground while building the 45th cutting – William Clark continued to ply his trade as a wagon-builder. His four daughters were the pride of his life; the story is told that each time any of the girls threatened to marry, their father would feign a heart-attack, and they would feel compelled to drop their matrimonial plans. Only the youngest daughter, Ethel, dared to call her father's bluff (the old man incidentally, lived, robustly, until well into his eighties), and in 1902 married a young Scot who, from all accounts, was a splendid and outstanding man.

Peter Miller Rattray, the son of a farmer in the Dalreoch area of Perthshire, Scotland, arrived in Durban in 1886 as a young boy, ready to seek his fortune with that tenacity and determination which characterized so many of the immigrants from an impoverished

William and Sarah Clark
married in 1859 (Colin Rattray)

160

Grandma Jee (Sarah's mother)
(Colin Rattray)

Tea in the garden at Camphill.
(Colin Rattray)

The Clark girls.
Ethel on the
right
(Colin Rattray)

Tennis party at Camphill. Peter Rattray
standing in centre of photograph
(Colin Rattray)

Scotland, which was suffering from the consequences of the industrial revolution. Peter soon established a contracting business and was ready, at the drop of a hat, to down tools and take up arms to fight for any colonial cause. In the Mashonaland Rebellion of 1896-1897 Peter was awarded a medal with clasp, being elevated to the rank of Captain.

The Duke of Athol, writing a tribute in a Scottish newspaper at the time of Peter's death in 1937, recounted how he, the Duke, was summoned to South Africa by Lord Kitchener to raise and command the Scottish Horse at the outbreak of the Anglo-Boer War. The Duke opened a tiny office in Pietermaritzburg, stuck a notice on the door and placed an advertisement in the local newspaper, asking for recruits. For two days there was no response. Then, recalled the Duke, in walked a tall burly farmer: 'There was something magnetic and something that gave you a great feeling of confidence in this splendid figure of a Scot whose outlook had been broaded by colonial experience' wrote the Duke, and continued that Rattray was 'a great athlete, a magnificent horseman, a dead shot, absolutely fearless…'. Rattray in no time helped the Duke to raise the men necessary to constitute the South African Squadron of the Scottish Horse.

No wonder Ethel lost her heart and defied her father to marry him. The Duke gave the bride away at their wedding in 1902.

Peter Rattray served gallantly and with distinction throughout the Boer War in the regiment where he was joined by three of his brothers. In the *Times History of the South African War* – 1900-1902, Vol V, p 382, there is mention of the significant part which Rattray played in a counter-attack which repulsed General de la Rey at Moedwil on September 30 1901. Captain Rattray was in command of the 'D' Squadron of the Scottish Horse. For his gallantry in the battle (during which both he and his brother David were wounded), Peter was awarded the DSO. In the course of the war he also received the Queen's medal with clasp and the King's medal with two clasps.

All the Rattray brothers (and there were nine of them) lived exciting and unusual lives. Brother Andrew had emigrated in 1897 to join the mounted police. He joined Peter and David in the Scottish Horse during

162

the Boer War, thereafter spending some time in the Argentine, and finally settled in Kenya, where he became a renowned hunter. On his farm outside Nairobi, he domesticated zebra, which he sent all over the world to zoos; he also fought a leopard to the death with his bare hands. With one hand he clutched the leopard's throat, and the other he thrust into the beast's mouth in an effort to suffocate him. This he managed to do, but was severely mauled in the process. His devoted native servants carried him over two hundred miles to Nairobi, where he received lengthy, but fortunately effective, medical treatment. Andrew became the white hunter to Lord Furness, shipping magnate and colliery owner. The Viscount's young daughter, The Hon Averill Furness, fell in love with the fifty-year old hunter, and they were secretly married. Father was furious and inserted the following advertisement in the *East African Standard*: 'To All Whom it May Concern – Take notice that from and after the twenty fourth day of January 1932 Mr A Rattray ceased to be the white hunter of my safari, and from that date he had no authority to order anything on my account.' The couple lived together in the bush

Peter Rattrays first home at Kwambonambi. 1912
(Colin Rattray)

until Andrew suddenly became ill and died. He was fifty-one – his wife was twenty-four. The story goes that Averill secluded herself alone in the bush and drank herself to an early death. The incident is recorded by Gloria Vanderbilt in her book *Double Exposure*.

Peter and Ethel's first son, Loring, was born in Sydenham, Durban in 1903. They had two more sons, Sylvester ('Pud') and Colin.

In 1912 Peter purchased 2 000 acres of barren farmland at Kwambonambi (about twenty kilometres north-west of the present Richard's Bay). He had ideas of cattle-ranching there, but although the area received a good annual rainfall, the soil was too sandy to be of any agricultural value.

At the outbreak of the Great War, despite his old war wounds, Peter joined up immediately. He saw service in Salonika, Egypt and France, and was commissioned Major.

During the war years Ethel stayed in Durban with her children.

Loring Rattray and his brother Sylvester ("Pud")

Ethel Rattray and her sons: Loring, Colin and "Pud". 1920

Loring attended Highbury School and then Durban High School. It was while her husband was away at the front that Ethel experimented by planting some Saligna gum seedlings in the sandy soil around the farmhouse on the Waterton Estate at Kwambonambi. These trees flourished, growing rapidly straight and tall, indicating that the climate and the sandy soil were ideal for growing gum trees. On his return, severely troubled by his war wounds and walking with the aid of crutches, Peter started his own Saligna nursery – the beginnings of what was to become a flourishing timber industry in Zululand. There is a story that Peter would limp across his lands on his crutches, followed by labourers who would pop seedling gum trees into the holes made by the crutches. Whether or not this is apocryphal, it certainly wasn't long before gum plantations stretched the length and breadth of Peter's Waterton Estate.

When young Loring left school, he worked as an office boy at George North & Son, a firm dealing in agricultural machinery. Later he worked for a motor firm, where he was taught the useful art of book-keeping. From there he moved to Mount Edgecombe to work at Natal Estates. Len Grice remembers working with him – they both received the princely wage of £6 a month.

In the early 1930s Loring, like many another Campbell employee, enjoyed a winter hunting trip to MalaMala at Wac's invitation. Loring was reputedly in great awe of the 'Makhulu Baas' – Wac Campbell – a feeling that was never to leave him.

In 1929 EP Masters (he of the tree at the Marthly water-hole) was fired from Natal Estates. Loring hoped for his job, but it was given instead to Alex Logan. Miffed, Loring gave the firm three months' notice. During that time, however, a vacancy occurred on the Blackburn Estate, which Loring was pleased to occupy.

Loring married Natalie Gazzard in 1931. A son, Michael, was born to the couple in 1932, and eleven years later, a daughter, Gail.

In 1937 Peter Rattray died of blackwater fever, which, with malaria, was one of the scourges of Zululand in those days. At the time of his death, Peter had 2 000 acres of maturing Saligna gums on his Waterton

Loring Rattray

Estate, and he also had other farms in Zululand. These he left to his son Loring.

The bushveld bug must have bitten Loring on that trip to MalaMala years previously for no sooner had he received his inheritance than he was journeying to the bushveld to investigate the possibility of buying a game farm. He stayed with the ranger at Toulon, and inspected the farm Exeter (on the north-west corner of the block) which he purchased for 7s/6d a morgen.

In the winter of that year, Loring's five-year old son, Michael, accompanied his father on a 'great trek' to the bushveld to see the new farm. It was quite an expedition. Loring's Cadillac led the procession followed by a one-ton truck, which in turn was followed by a five-ton lorry. The vehiches overflowed with wide-eyed Zulus (who had never before travelled beyond the borders of their native Zululand), crates of chickens, dogs and food. The journey took five days. Somehow, along the way, the dogs broke into the crates of chickens, half of which they devoured. Loring, furious, shot two of the dogs. The young Mike, amusing himself by playing on his newly-acquired mouth-organ, had the mortification of seeing his precious instrument hurled from the car window by his irate father, where it joined the corpses of the dogs on the side of the road. It was a very jaded party which arrived at Toulon, where the hospitality of Leo and Esmé Lownds helped restore some of Loring's equilibrium. The following morning they trekked to Exeter. Two years later Loring bought the farm Wallingford, which lies to the south of Exeter for one guinea a morgen.

Loring inherited not only his father's farms, but also his drive and determination to develop timber-related industries in Zululand. After the 1939-1945 war, tests which Peter had initiated before his death were completed under Loring's guidance; tests which proved that the Saligna grown in Zululand was suitable for the production of cellulose. This led to the establishment of a cellulose plant in Umkomaas, Natal, a site which was chosen because of the availability of plentiful water. The plant consumed over 160 000 tons of saligna timber a year. Other industries followed: a hardboard factory was opened in Verulam, a

166

paper factory at Tugela, and sawmills at Kwambonambi. Loring's pioneering work in timber in Zululand gained recognition when he was, understandably, made Life-President of the South African Timber Growers' Association. His farming enterprises were not, however, limited to timber; he successfuly farmed sugar, pineapples (and had an interest in a large canning factory at Empangeni and Zululand), cotton, cattle and sisal. He also ventured into the budding South African ship-building industry, providing finance, with other backers, for a company which led to the launching of the coaster 'Tugela' in 1968.

When old William Clark died in 1918, he bequeathed both the Pine Street and the Camphill properties to the Mayor and Councillors of Durban in perpetual trust for the erection of a home for destitute children, as well as for recreation and pleasure grounds. Each year a scholarship for a boy and a girl was also provided for. Until their deaths, Clark's daughters, and after them his grandsons, should have usufruct of the estate. Clark's three spinster daughters, always known as 'the girls', lived in the old family home at Camphill until their deaths, (they all died in 1943). Ethel Rattray had died at a much younger age than her sisters, at fifty-eight in 1934. In 1964, Loring and Colin (the only two surviving brothers) anticipated the terms of their grandfather's will, and had the Children's Home and the William Clark Gardens constructed.

Each winter Loring and Natalie, together with their family and friends, visited the lowveld game farms. At first Exeter and Wallingford were used for hunting, but later Loring's interest was in conservation, to which he brought the same drive and enthusiasm with which he had pursued his other farming ventures.

In 1950 the Transvaal Land Owners Association, which had undertaken the administration of the Sabi Private Game Scheme since 1934, was liquidated, and its functions were assumed by a newly-formed association of landowners which was named the Sabi Sand Wildtuin. From the first, Loring played a significant part in the organization, and was present at the inaugural meeting which was held at MalaMala.

In 1961 he began experimenting with the re-introduction of some

167

species of game which had become extinct in the area. He enclosed a 400 morgen camp with a vermin-proof fence – known as the 'Rhino Park' – and here he introduced ostriches, eland and white rhino. Only the latter flourished. Today, thanks to his foresight, finance and energy, the Sabi Sand area abounds with these animals.

Once the Kruger Park completed the veterinary fence which forms the eastern boundary of the Sabi Sand Wildtuin, it was decided by the owners to fence the entire area. Seventy-five miles of six-foot fence was erected, enclosing an area of 265 square miles. Because game could no longer migrate from the Kruger Park, the owners realized the importance of formulating a co-operative policy of wild-life management, which all owners would be compelled to follow.

Loring's great contribution to the Sabi Sand Wildtuin, and this is acknowledged by the more thoughtful and bush-conscious of his fellow members, was as a conservationist. He believed in applying good farming principles to the game farms, which would be to the benefit of not only his own, but everyone's interests. He envisaged the area as a whole, and persuaded members that a team effort was needed, and that conservation and careful game management would be to everyone's advantage, and, what was of more importance, to the advantage of the bush and the animals.

Loring initiated game counts. In the dry season, when most of the owners were visiting their farms, it was arranged that each owner should position himself by day at a water-hole, and make an estimation of numbers of game as they came to drink. Loring also generously provided, at his own expense, an aircraft, from which an aerial game survey could be undertaken; only one of many instances when he put his hand into his pocket for the benefit of the group.

In 1956 a quota system for hunting was introduced, whereby members' hunting requirements were examined by an executive committee, who then issued permits. It had been decided by the committee that as the numbers of lions were decreasing, no lionesses were permitted to be shot. Loring was at this time Chairman of the committee, and as such had to deal with complaints and violations of

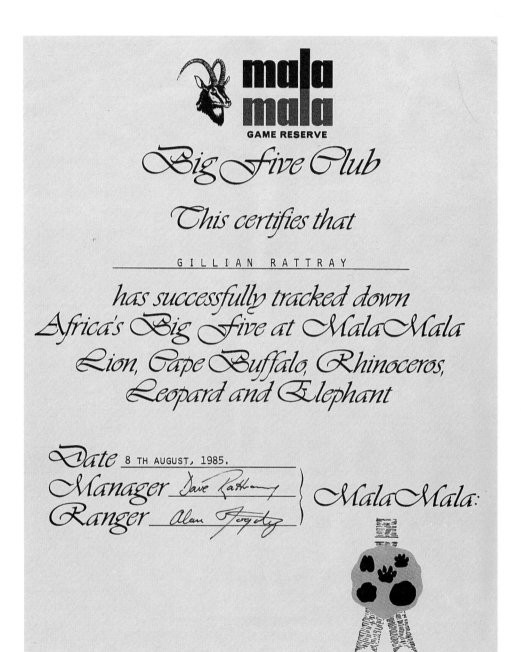

mala mala
GAME RESERVE

Big Five Club

This certifies that

GILLIAN RATTRAY

has successfully tracked down
Africa's Big Five at MalaMala
Lion, Cape Buffalo, Rhinoceros,
Leopard and Elephant

Date 8 TH AUGUST, 1985.
Manager Dave Rattray
Ranger Alan Forgsly   *MalaMala:*

Big Five certificate - granted to a visitor to
malamala who sees: Lion, elephant, Cape buffalo,
white Rhino and leopard.

regulations. It was brought to the committee's notice that Wac Campbell had shot two lionesses. Loring, as Chairman, had to act on the information. He had never lost the fear of Wac which he had had as a young employee at Natal Estates. So Loring took the easy way out. He wrote Wac a letter of complaint, and instructed his son Michael to deliver it to the old man who was staying, as usual, at MalaMala. Michael flew there in his plane, landing on the airstrip which used to run on the flat area between the camp and the flood plain of the river. Campbell was asleep in a large grass chair in front of the fire in the boma, a balaclava cap protecting his grizzled head from the wintery air. Mike timidly woke the old chap, and nervously presented him with Loring's letter. After reading it Wac looked at the young man: 'Go back to your father, young man, and tell him that my eyesight is failing – I thought the beasts were males', he declared. As Wac had killed the animals at 300 yards with open sights, and with one shot each, his reply was treated with scepticism!

During Loring's chairmanship, he persuaded the members to agree not to shoot any lion for a period of one year. This helped to restore the imbalance which had developed between antelope and predator.

The general attitude towards conservation was becoming more positive and the efforts of the members were being rewarded in a general increase of game on their farms. Not only was the increase in numbers. Animals which had hitherto not been seen in the Sabi Sand were appearing. In 1950 the first giraffe were seen coming across the river at Marthly; in 1953 the first hippo was seen disporting itself in the deep pool in the Sand river, where now dozens make their permanent home; that same year an elephant was seen for the first time on the farm Toulon, the fore-runner of many pioneer bull elephants.

Loring had mentioned to Urban Campbell that if MalaMala was ever on the market, he would like first option. In 1964 Urban telephoned Rattray's office to offer him his farm for sale. Loring was overseas at the time. Mike remembers taking the call and relaying the information to his father, who did not take long to conclude the deal. The transfer of MalaMala took place in November that year.

It was only when Loring bought MalaMala from Urban that he foresaw the possibilities of extending the operation which Urban had begun, and of marketing MalaMala as a top-rate tourist attraction. He closed the camp for six months while he built the dining room, bar, garages and laundry and extended the accommodation. From the start he sought to blend the buildings with the bush as much as possible, so that the camp and operation should impinge as minimally as possible on the environment. He employed rangers, purchased game-viewing vehicles, and constructed hides in the bush, well away from the camp – high platforms in the trees, where at night bait was put for lions below the trees, and with the aid of spotlights, guests could enjoy watching the lions feed while they enjoyed their evening drinks.

The services of a top-rate chef, named Romeo, were procured, who performed gastronomic miracles in the up-dated kitchens. A multi-racial staff was employed: Indian barmen were brought from Natal, local black men and women found welcome all-year-round employment at the camp. The old faithful tracker Tayi Mhlaba became Loring's chief tracker.

Although Loring at first encountered the same flak with which Urban had been bombarded when he began his commercial enterprise, epithets such as 'sacrilege' soon ceased to be bandied about by members of the Sabi Sand Wildtuin, as they were reassured that Loring did not intend to exploit the bush. Making money was a secondary consideration, and although during Loring's lifetime MalaMala became a byword in international tourist circles, and was visited by people of consequence from all over the world, it always ran at a loss.

In TV Bulpin's *Discovering South Africa*, (1970), MalaMala is described thus:

Luxurious accommodation for up to 22 people... tariff of R30 per day includes guides, transport, very fine food and the thrill of watching big game from tree-top hides.

R30 in today's terms seems ludicrously low – a five-star hotel in the

Gina Lollabrigida
with Loring Rattray.
1960's

Mike Rattray, centre
with Jack Nicklaus
and Gary Player. 1966

Jimmy Connors and
his wife Patty

a' Malamala

General Haig (U.S.A) flanked
by David and Mike Rattray,
in the 1970's

Moyshe Dayan

Sir Laurens van der Post
a' Malamala. 1983

same year charged R12 bed-and-breakfast.

Loring died in February 1975, at the age of seventy-one, leaving his wife with the usufruct of the estate. His son, Michael, acquired the MalaMala business and approximately 7 000 acres from his father's estate, with borrowed capital.

At this time Michael, in his early forties, was himself a vigorous and successful businessman and farmer in his own right. Like his father, he had a spread of interests, and like his father he was equipped with imagination to formulate objectives and the energy, enthusiasm and intelligence necessary for their attainment.

Mike, also like his father, was a fine horseman, a good shot, altogether an outdoor person. And he had always loved the bush. Although his immediate plan regarding MalaMala was to endeavour to turn what had been a financial loss into at least a break-even enterprise, it never entered his mind to sacrifice any of his father's principles in so doing.

Mike at once increased the tariff and the accommodation. The former he doubled, which led to a roar of protest from the travel agents: 'This is the talk of Johannesburg' wailed an irate agent. But, as Mike had anticipated, the fact that 'everyone' was talking about it proved to be the finest advertising he could have wished for. The occupancy rate went up the following month. Mike increased the accommodation to fifty beds, a figure which he had carefully considered. Fifty guests fill a bus, a Comair aeroplane, and fit snugly into travel arrangements. The staff was also increased. A maximum of fifty guests would be cared for by one hundred and fifty members of staff – a staggering ratio. Although this would mean that the tariff would have to be high, Mike Rattray believed that it would be better to have less people paying more than more people paying less. Underlying this belief is his philosophy that human 'pollution' should be kept at the lowest possible level, and that it should be as concentrated as possible. Thus it is at MalaMala that of the five farms which make up the 50 000 acres of the enterprise, only on two of the farms – MalaMala and Toulon – are there buidings of any

174

description. The impact of people on the natural environment is thus kept to an absolute minimum.

A government commission was undertaken in 1977 to determine the viability of an enterprise such as MalaMala in terms of usage and productivity of land. It was concluded that the contribution which the MalaMala enterprise made to the country in terms of foreign earnings far exceeded the income which the land could generate if it were run as an agricultural undertaking.

In 1975 the Sabi Sand Wildtuin celebrated the twenty-fifth year of its existence as an association. It was sad that Loring had not lived long enough to share in the celebration, as he had taken such an active and meaningful part in its formation and existence. He would have been proud that his son, as Vice-Chairman, offered to have MalaMala as the venue for the festivities. More than 350 guests gathered on the banks of the Sand river, beside the swimming pool. The guests included the ex-State President, Jim Fouché and his wife, the Prime Minister John Vorster and his wife, the Administrator of the Transvaal, various ambassadors, office-bearers and members of wild-life societies and National Parks Boards, as well as the members of the Sabi Sand and their friends. A Boere-orkes (type of homespun band) provided the music; traditional bushveld food there was in abundance; liquor flowed. In the early hours of the next morning the guests gathered up their chairs (which they had been requested to bring) climbed (some unsteadily) into their vehicles, and made off in the dark for their various destinations. A seven-year old boy was found asleep beside the camp-fire next morning, and one of the guests from a neighbouring farm opened up her folded chair to discover in it: a squashed melk-tert, a lady's handbag, a bunch of car keys and an air-ticket. It had been a memorable evening!

There have been other celebrations through the years at MalaMala. In 1980 the new airstrip was completed and a grand opening took place exactly forty-three years after the first plane had landed on Urban Campbell's old airstrip at Eyrefield. (It had been then that one of the black trackers, old Zaba, had asked the unforgettable question: 'When

that bird has a baby, can I have one?') The pilot of the 1937 plane had
been a man called Noel Carbutt. Now forty-three years later, the new
airstrip was opened by Carbutt's son Edward, himself a pilot, and co-
incidentally, forty-three years old. The finest champagne and kudu
biltong were consumed by the guests who stood in the midday sun on
what must be one of the most picturesque landing strips anywhere:
fringed with bush, overlooking the path of the river, with a panoramic
view of the bushveld beyond. And what other airstrip can boast a family
of resident warthogs?

There have been sad times too at MalaMala: years of bitter drought –
in 1970 and again in 1983 when all the staff could do was stand helplessly
by, watching nature's most cruel culling process at work; when waterholes became hard, caked with cement-like mud; when the Sand river
ceased to flow; when the bush stank with the rotting of hundreds of
animal carcasses; when only a few of the fittest survived. But good
game and conservation practices paid off, and these, when the good
rains fell once more, ensured that the bush and the game rapidly and

miraculously recovered within a season.

Although MalaMala is fundamentally a business enterprise run on sound principles, its success depends also on good veld and game management. Like his father before him, Mike insists on a scientific approach being adopted; the ecology is studied and understood. Each week a ranger is required to read a paper on some aspect of animal or bush interest to the other rangers, a task which requires a good deal of observation and research. Thus the knowledge at MalaMala is continually expanding.

Careful game and weather reports are kept; new bush-clearing techniques are tried; game counts are regularly undertaken; culling is done on a highly scientific basis. MalaMala has official assistance from the Transvaal Department of Nature Conservation; unofficial contact is maintained with the ever-helpful staff of the Kruger National Park; animal and botanical investigations and studies are frequently undertaken. Mike Rattray was appointed to the Board of Trustees of the National Parks Board in 1984.

A technical staff is employed to keep the wheels of the MalaMala machinery turning. A full-time mechanic services the fleet of landrovers, buses, jeeps, tractors, road-making and fire-fighting equipment. There is a resident electrician. In the old days the water for the camp was hand-pumped from the river. Today electrically-driven machinery performs the task, although the man in charge is the same old Shangaan whose sing-song voice could be heard all day long as he sang a rhythmical accompaniment to his pumping in the Campbell days. Old Chamus Indhlovu – Chumps, as he is known to everyone – is still in the water business, though in his (very) old age he has been elevated to the post of overseer.

Supplies no longer come from the Newington Store, or by the Selati line from Komatipoort: a truck twice-weekly fetches stores from Nelspruit. No longer are wordy telegrams misspelt and despatched by the postmaster at Acornhoek: now messages fly back and forth by telex and telephone. Two radio networks operate throughout the night and day.

Mike Rattray and Harry Kukman. 1983

A well-equipped boutique offers the guest fine luxury goods made in South Africa.

Although MalaMala is in one way in the middle of nowhere, it is also the centre of a little world of its own. But always there is the bush, upon which the modern improvements are not permitted to intrude. In fact the opposite is the case; it is not unusual for a buck to wander through the camp, or a mongoose, or a civet cat. A family of persistent warthogs is frequently chased across the lawn and back into the bush. A hippo once chose to take a dip in the camp swimming pool – monkeys and baboons are frequent, if not always welcome, visitors. And always there are the birds…

In 1983 Mike Rattray purchased the farm Toulon, which lies in the south-eastern corner of the Sabi Sand, bordering on the Kruger Park near Skukuza. Mike has, in the ten years since his father's death entirely with his own resources, increased the Mala-Mala enterprise five-fold.

Toulon had belonged to the Roche family who had bought it from Mrs Mary Whitehead in 1945. The earliest record of ownership in the Transvaal Deeds Office was 1870, when Toulon was given as a quitrent farm to John Gavin King. Thereafter it had several owners, a notable one being Hugo Nellmapius, who bought it in 1889. On his death it was acquired by the Landed Property Co Ltd, which sold it in 1902 to the Transvaal Consolidated Land and Exploration Company (TCL). They ranched cattle on Toulon in the 1920s, selling the farm eventually to Mrs Hall (who became Whitehead) in 1934.

The Roche's old family home, which had been lovingly cared for by its owners, was converted most tastefully and successfully into a new camp which could accommodate twenty guests. Norma Rattray transformed the buildings, decorating them in Victorian style, so that the camp has an atmosphere of old-world charm and history.

It was decided to name the camp after Harry Kirkman, whose home had been at Toulon for many years, when he had been the TCL ranger from 1927-1933, and later (after a period when Harry had been employed by the Kruger Park) as the Sabi Sand Wildtuin ranger from 1959 to 1969. It seemed fitting that this wonderful character of the bush

179

Harry Kirkman. Kirkman's Kamp is named in his honour.

should be honoured in such a way. Harry's faithful old gun rests in a glass case in the camp sitting-room, and his portrait graces the place of honour above the fireplace.

Sir Lourens van der Post, that world-famous South African writer and man of the bush, was invited to open Kirkman's Camp on November 28 1983. In a moving speech he stressed the importance of conservation in the modern world. Getting close to nature, he

Mike and Norma Rattray. 1986
(Dennis Cleaver)

maintained, was necessary for man's very survival, not only in a physical, but more important, in a spiritual sense. Man, which he considers is the most endangered species, needs to commune with the wilderness if he is to preserve his wholeness. Sir Lourens commended Mike and Norma Rattray for their continuing efforts to conserve and preserve wild life and the environment for the benefit of others.

In 1983 Andrew Harper's *Hideaway Report* had rated MalaMala as one of the world's top twenty-three 'hideaways' (the only one on the continent of Africa). Two years later MalaMala was given the singular honour as the top Safari Lodge in the world. While such recognition crowns the Rattrays' efforts to maintain a high level of excellence in running MalaMala, this excellence was not at the expense of the exploitation of the environment, for in 1983 Mike Rattray was the recipient of the coveted award for conservation, made annually by the Transvaal province – the Ossie Doyer Award. Surely no man could ask for more than these twin awards to crown his efforts. Not only has MalaMala put South Africa firmly on the international tourist map, but perhaps of more worth is that 50 000 acres of precious wilderness are being nurtured and preserved with expertise and with dedication.

Somehow Mike and Norma Rattray have struck the magical balance between a superbly run business venture, and a scientifically conserved wilderness.

Malamala camp today

The boma

Guest accommodation.

183

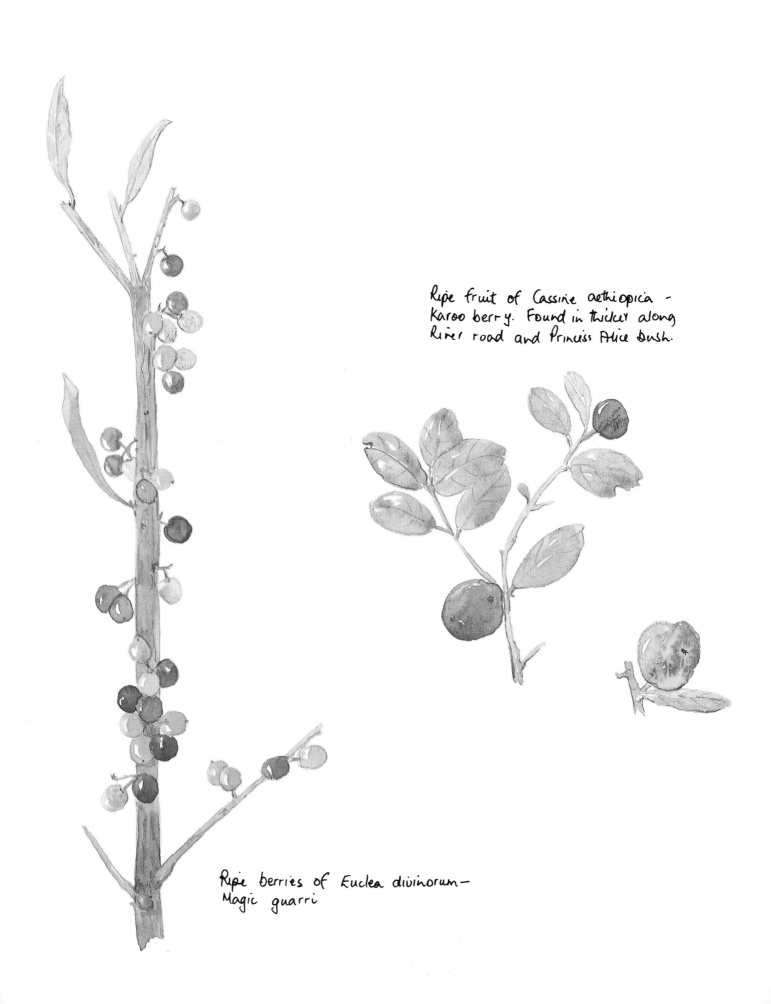

Ripe fruit of Cassine aethiopica -
Karoo berry. Found in thicket along
River road and Princess Alice Bush.

Ripe berries of Euclea divinorum -
Magic guarri

Russel-backed Sand frog.
Tomopterna marmorata

AUTUMN

Blue Waterlily -
Nymphae caerula.
Delicately fragrant.
(size reduced)

'… there is a harmony in autumn, and a lustre in the sky …'
Shelley,   *The Indian Serenade*

Autumn anywhere is a period both of maturing and of preparation. In
the bushveld there is a sense that nature is settling back and resting after
her summer endeavour of ensuring that all species will continue. If the
summer rains have been good, the abundant veld seems to hug to itself
its maturing goodness and life-giving energy. The sap sinks in the
deciduous trees, and the leaves turn and begin to fall. Pods and berries
ripen. There is much activity where the Magic guarrie bushes are laden
with the tiny raisin-sweet fruit, which is the delight of monkeys,
baboons, birds and elephants, and even rangers (in passing).

   Although autumn at MalaMala is the beginning of the dry season,
there is water still in most of the waterholes and dams; in some, lilies
bloom pale blue, and perfume the air with their delicate fragrance.
Insects and bees are drawn to these late summer blooms, relishing the
nectar, rolling in the pollen which is carried on the pointed ends of rows
of stamens. Mud there is in abundance for the warthogs, whose
wallowing cools their plump bodies, and helps to rid their hides of those
parasites which the ever-present oxpeckers have not
devoured. Frogs will soon burrow deep down beneath the
surface mud and begin the shallow minimal breathing
which makes it possible for them to hibernate there with
little oxygen and no food.

Old male warthog at
Mamba waterhole

Impala rams in rut

Fallen leaves of the Round-leafed kiaat.

Leaves of Round-leafed kiaat

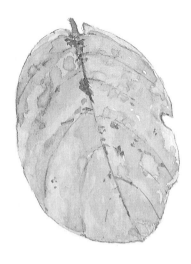

Leaves of Combretum zeyheri -
Large-fruited bushwillow.

Yellow Pansy ♂
Junonia hierta cebrene

Autumn is not only a preparation for the 'little death' of winter, but a time when next summer's seed is sown. The impala rut in the autumn, and the males are occupied with establishing their territories and their supremacy within the herd. There is a sound of clashing horns, and a strange snorting which sounds quite lion-like. (Our ranger was clearly not believed when he assured some nervous guests who stood in the veld sipping their sundown drinks, that the 'roars' heard were impala and not lion.). We watched a stately impala ram, already established as lord of his harem, mark his territory by rubbing his forehead against the grass (so that tiny glands there could secrete his particular scent), and trot bossily after some errant females, bringing them back into the body of the herd. A MalaMala employee, checking on the roads in the north, came across a dying impala ram whose lung had been fatally pierced by a fellow male who stood nearby with blood still on the tips of his horns. The victor and vanquished would doubtless have browsed happily beside each other in the bachelor herd until the shorter autumn days somehow triggered a surge of hormones which resulted in this aggressive behaviour. Not only does this ensure that the finest genetic material will be transmitted to the future generation, but the males' ruttish behaviour causes the females' hormones to react, making them receptive to the 'superior' male.

Other animals are marking their territory; we saw a huge male rhino, plastered from head to toe in pale grey mud, mark his domain by spraying on some bushes. We drove over to inspect his 'mark' – the pungent urine was thick and milky. (A guest remarked that the rhino seemed to need the attention of a urologist). This is all part of nature's way – the animal's world is made up of smell-messages and instinctive commands which are disobeyed at peril.

Elephants can still find sufficient greenery to make up the gigantic 200

188

Square-lipped –
White – rhino

The last of the berries of the Buffalo thorn. Tiny new leaves had been encouraged by some late summer rain.

kilograms which is their daily average intake. We watched a lone bull-elephant tearing bark from a large marula tree. Using always his right tusk which was the one he favoured (it was worn much shorter than the left), he felt the tree with the sensitive end of his trunk, selecting an area which appealed to him. Then using the tip of his trunk he guided his tusk under the bark, piercing it and stripping it off upwards, leaving a bare raw redness on the tree's trunk. The elephant then took hold of the loose flap of bark with his trunk, placing it sideways into his mouth. While he munched, he rested his head against the tree.

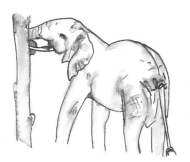

Elephants have been digging holes in the dry river beds to obtain fresh water which will filter through the sand, which they find preferable to the muddy liquid residue in some of the waterholes. These great holes will serve another purpose when the spring rains come to fill them; turtles, frogs and water-insects will make their home there. In such a pool we once spotted the tiny projecting tips of the periscope-like antennae of a water-scorpion who can stay under the water indefinitely using this marvellous appendage to draw breath. In the bed of the dry Mlowathi stream, near one of the elephant holes, an empty freshwater mussel shell lay, discarded by a Cape Clawless otter, whose dinner it had made. In the steep cliff-bank of the river, White-fronted bee-eaters had fashioned their nest holes last spring.

At the long pool in the Sand river, hippo wallow in the warm deep river, and a crocodile lies half-out of the water on a rock, enjoying the sun's warmth. A darter (aptly-named 'snake bird') swims upstream, its body completely submerged, its neck swaying like a snake about to

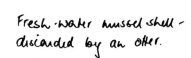

Fresh-water mussel shell — discarded by an otter.

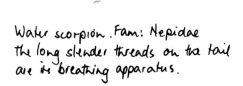

Water scorpion. Fam: Nepidae the long slender threads on the tail are its breathing apparatus.

Pods of Acacia welwitschii – Delagoa thorn.
The only ones left by the giraffe – the thorny
tree had to be climbed to reach them.

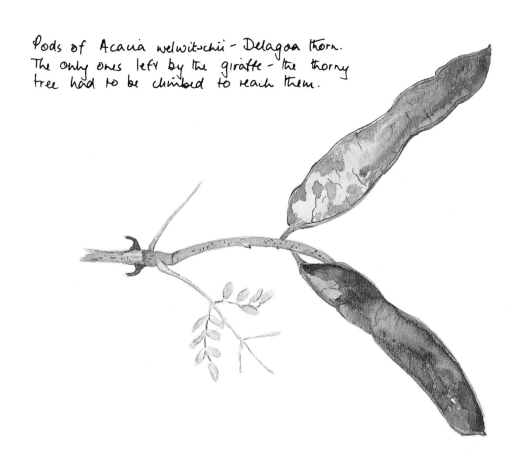

Pods of Acacia senegal – Slender
three-hook thorn.

Wild sage

Growing in riverine bush. Once in water
at camp the tiny flowerets began to open —
cerise stamens appeared. The flowers are
slightly prickly. I think they become those
beastly things which stick in your socks.

Paper-wasp nest anchored
firmly in the hollow of the
leaf of a Red rock-fig.

The Darter stretches its wings, drying its feathers in the afternoon sun.

A Darter on a rock in the Sand river

strike. Later the large bird stands, wings outstretched, on a rock in the river, drying its black and white feathers.

This is the time of year to see the amazing spectacle of the processional caterpillars: larvae of Anaphe reticulata or Reticulate Bagnest moth. We saw the hairy caterpillars on their way to have a final gorge on one of their favourite foodplants, the Jacket plum, before they congregate in their composite silken nests to undergo the miraculous metamorphosis, changing from creeping caterpillar to elegant brown and white moths. The caterpillars always march in a long, continuous line, which sometimes extends for many metres. If disturbed, they will mill about for a while, and then re-form. We came across several of these processions, once stopping only just in time, and deviating into the bush to avoid running through the line. It is assumed that moving in this way serves as a protection against predators, who imagine that they are seeing one *long* creature. Several bare-stemmed Jacket plum branches bore testimony to the fact that dozens of hungry caterpillars had fed there. But although damage was certainly wreaked on the bushes, the

192

Waterbuck female

Termite mound built against
a *Schotia brachypetala* tree

thick layer of black caterpillar droppings on the ground beneath was replenishing the earth with goodness.

The termites forage busily at this time of year. These marvellous creatures, whose clay homes rise like towers in the bush, belong to an incredibly organized and perfectly-run social system. The towers are perfect examples of engineering and air-conditioning skills. Each mound (and some are reputedly over 2 000 years old) is constructed from particles of soil cemented together by the insects' saliva and droppings. The latter are the end-product of a process whereby the cellulose in the termites' food (which they are not able to digest completely) is passed through the digestive system of one insect after another until all the nourishment has been absorbed. The brownish paste-like droppings are used both in building and in the making of the fungus-gardens, which the garden-workers tend in 'cellars' within the

Ripe marula berries

Two old buffaloes - kicked out by
the herd

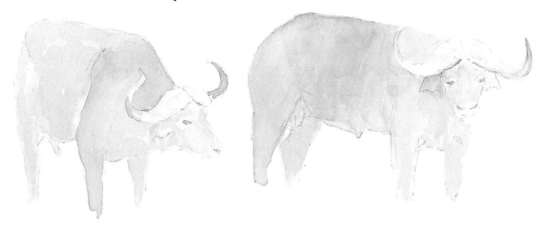

Waterbuck bull

Crocs basking in the sun at
the Hippo pool.

Kudu female

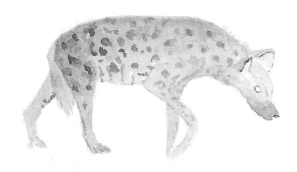

Spotted hyena loping down the
road at dusk - eyes shining in the
light of our vehicle.

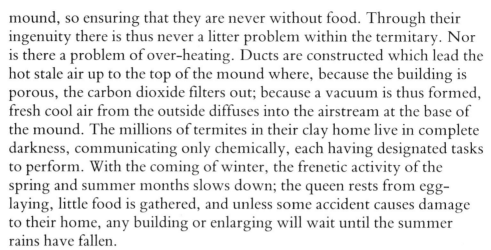

Pods of Combretum apiculatum –
Red bushwillow

mound, so ensuring that they are never without food. Through their ingenuity there is thus never a litter problem within the termitary. Nor is there a problem of over-heating. Ducts are constructed which lead the hot stale air up to the top of the mound where, because the building is porous, the carbon dioxide filters out; because a vacuum is thus formed, fresh cool air from the outside diffuses into the airstream at the base of the mound. The millions of termites in their clay home live in complete darkness, communicating only chemically, each having designated tasks to perform. With the coming of winter, the frenetic activity of the spring and summer months slows down; the queen rests from egg-laying, little food is gathered, and unless some accident causes damage to their home, any building or enlarging will wait until the summer rains have fallen.

Above the earth the snakes are active. We see their tracks zig-zagging across the roads. The reptiles are busy searching for food which will see them through their winter hibernation. We watched a Vine snake (Thelotornis capensis), its body bulging just behind its head, being attacked by a pair of bulbulls. The birds dived and pecked in a frantic but vain attempt to rescue their offspring which the snake had just swallowed.

Some birds have already left MalaMala and have migrated to warmer climes. No longer does the trill of the Woodland kingfisher ring out from every corner of the bush. The Spottedback weavers have abandoned their colony of hanging nests in the great marula trees at the camp; the cuckoos are preparing to leave; the Steppe eagles have already returned to their native Asia and the Wahlberg's eagles will soon wing their way north and westward to winter elsewhere. The Lesser-striped swallows who swooped and dived over the river in the late afternoons, have gathered for the last time on the boom at the side of the bridge, and have left for Europe. So have some of the storks, although the Marabous, those quaint ugly birds, so like undertakers walking with their hands behind their backs, can still be seen, usually in pairs, hunched on the branches of some dead leadwood trees. Heuglin's robins still sing their delightful songs in the thick bush by the river, near the

Marabou stork. Looking like an
undertaker - hands behind his back.

Heuglin's robin - one of the bushveld's
finest songsters - calling as the sun
was setting.

The leaves of the Wild Grape have turned to crimson

West Street waterhole, where the turning leaves of the Wild grape (Rhoicissus tomentose) flash crimson on the vines.

The early morning drives begin after an early breakfast in the autumn. The air is fresh; there is a nip in the air. Woolly scarves and caps are donned for at least the first hour of the drive in the open vehicles. Dew hangs heavy on the grass. In an area where the fluffy Eragrostis grass grows in profusion, the rising sun's rays catch the dew-clad flowerheads, turning the place into a white fairyland. Gossamer bowls of cobwebs hold the shimmering dew drops in their hollows. Other webs are flat in shape, strung between the thorny branches of the acacia saplings, or between stalks of sturdy grass. All beautifully fashioned during the night by industrious spiders, hoping to catch some hapless insect prey. The autumn morning at MalaMala is a wonderland of tiny dew stars. In the deep shade, where the warming sun has not yet penetrated, I see an African Monarch butterfly, wings close together, still sleeping on a blade of grass.

As the earth colour changes, so does the vegetation. The silver Terminalia trees (Terminalia sericea) take the place of the Combretums on the edge of the seeplines; pinkish-grey pods hang among the silver

197

Mother and son

Green berries of Buffalo thorn -
Ziziphus mucronata

Ripe fruit of Sanseviera hyacinthoides -
mother-in-law's tongue.

Malvaceae sp.

Straggly compositae sp. which
grows in the thick grass. Could
be an invader.

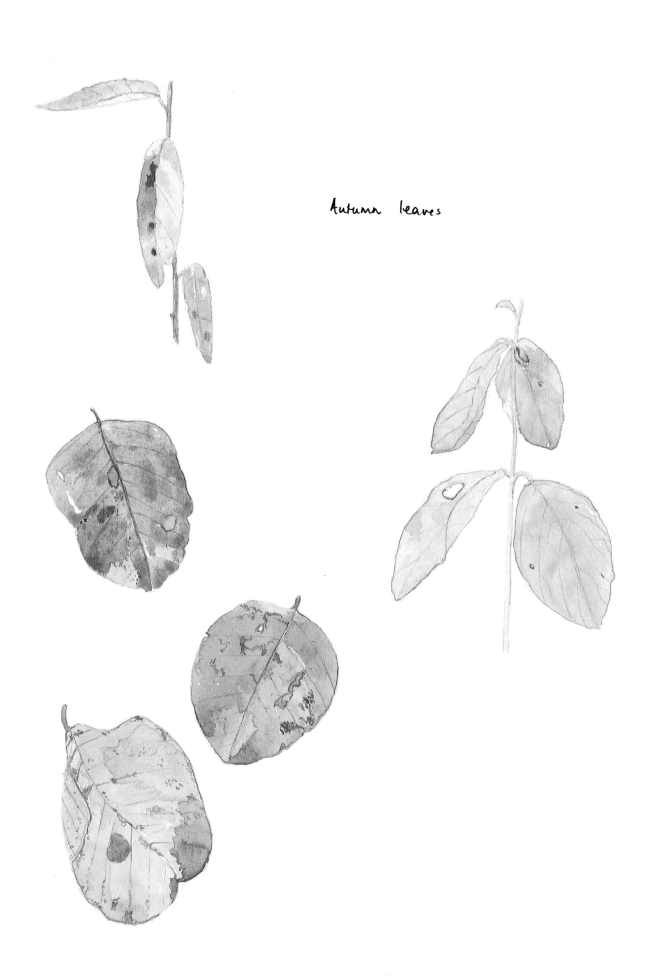

Autumn leaves

leaves. Where the ground becomes stonier, the Round-leafed kiaat (Pterocarpus rotundifolius) flourishes. Some of their shiny leaves have already turned to red and gold. A male Coqui francolin, its neck a warm ochre, its back beautifully patterned in black and white, searches among the fallen leaves for the seeds and insects on which it feeds. Like other game birds, the francolins use carbohydrate as their source of energy. We are told that, because of this, and because of their comparatively large bodyweight, the francolin's flight is of short duration.

At the Buffalo pans the tambotie trees are in full autumnal splendour, their oblong leaves a glory of orange and red. Pods of the Dwarf Schotia (Schotia capitata) hang from the grey stumpy branches.

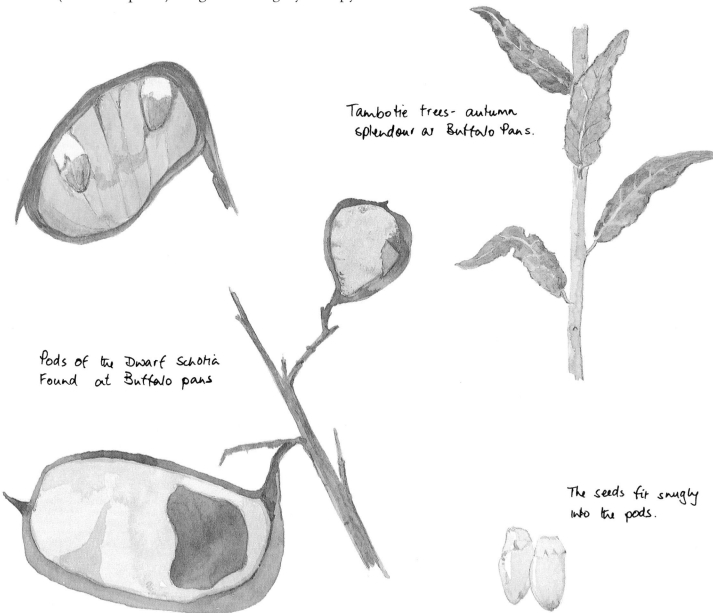

Tambotie trees- autumn splendour at Buffalo Pans.

Pods of the Dwarf Schotia Found at Buffalo pans

The seeds fit snugly into the pods.

Transvaal saffron -
Cassine transvaalensis.
in David's garden at
camp.

Commiphora neglecta - Sweet-root corkwood. Growing
near 'Reception' in the camp.

Euclea divinorum

Kalanchoe lanceolata

Mistletoe - Tapinanthus kraussianus
subsp. transvaalensis. (Formerly Loranthus)

Nymphoides thunbergia - Yellow water lily.
Growing in the stagnant water at the
mamba waterhole

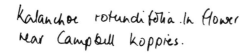

Kalanchoe rotundifolia. In flower
near Campbell koppies.

The shadows of the tall knob-thorn trees lengthen, and the impala move into open areas so that they can more effectively watch for predators. Zebras call – an almost urgent watery sound, which is one of the haunting bush noises. As we cross the river we stop in the sand beside the water, and watch a male giraffe bending low to drink. Our view is from behind; the animal's head is hidden in some reeds. Our tracker cannot contain his mirth at the ludicrous picture which the giraffe presents. We enjoy another amusing incident later, when the sun has set. Our spotlight picks out a number of baboons sleeping high in the branches of a thorn tree, which overhangs the road. The strong light disturbs the animals who, with a great to-do tumble in disarray from their perches. Leaves, branches and baboons of all sizes seem to rain down from above. The animals pick themselves up and make off in panic into the bush. Our laughter echoes into the night.

The Sand river - at West Street waterhole.

IN CONCLUSION

And so the seasons pass at MalaMala, each with its own accents, tones and colours, all contributing in perfect harmony to Nature's purpose: the continuation of the species.

While man wreaks havoc on the world around him, here, thanks to the care and dedication of its preservers, Nature holds dominion; here we can still observe and wonder at her marvellous ways and refresh our souls with her peace.

BIBLIOGRAPHY

Abery, LS (ed). *The Times History of the War in South Africa 1899-1902, Vols IV & V*.
   Sampson Low, Marston & Co Ltd: London 1906/7
Bulpin, TV. *Low Veld Trails*. Books of Africa: Cape Town, 1968
   Lost Trails of the Low Veld. Books of Africa: Cape Town, 1969
   Discovering South Africa. Books of Africa: Cape Town, 1970
Cartwright, AP. *The Corner House*. Purnell & Sons: Cape Town. 1965
   The First South African. Purnell & Sons: Cape Town, 1971
   Valley of Gold. Purnell & Sons: Cape Town, 1973
   Transvaal Lowveld. Purnell & Sons: Cape Town, 1978
Clancey, PA. *Gamebirds of Southern Africa*. Purnell & Sons: Cape Town, 1967
Dickson, CG & Kroon, M (eds). *Pennington's Butterflies of Southern Africa*.
   Ad Donker: Johannesburg, 1978
Fabian, Anita & Germishuizen, Gerritt. *Transvaal Wild Flowers*. MacMillan:
   Johannesburg, 1982
Fitzpatrick, JP. *The Transvaal From Within*. Heineman: London, 1900
   Jock of the Bushveld. Longmans: London, 1920
Herd, Norman. *Killie's Africa*. Blue Crane Books: Pietermaritzburg, 1982
Kaye, Helga. *The Tycoon and the President. The Life and Times of
   Alois Hugo Nellmapius 1847-1893*. MacMillan: Johannesburg, 1978
Kloppers, Hannes. *Game Ranger*. Juta: Cape Town, 1970
Kloppers, Johannes & van Son. G. *Butterflies of the Kruger National Park*. National Parks
   Board: Pretoria, 1978
Levin, Branch Rappoport & Mitchell. *A Field Guide to the Mushrooms of South Africa*.
   Struik: Cape Town, 1985
Meiring, Piet. *Behind the Scenes in the Kruger Park*. Perskor: Johannesburg, 1982
Newman, Kenneth. *Birdlife in Southern Africa*. MacMillan: Johannesburg, 1971
   Birds of Southern Africa 1. Kruger National Park. MacMillan: Johannesburg, 1980
Onderstall, Jo *South African Wild Flower Guide: Transvaal Lowveld & Escarpment* (1984)
Osborne, RF. *Valiant Harvest*. South African Sugar Association, 1964
Passmore & Carruthers *South African Frogs* Wits Univerity Press: Johannesburg, 1979
Pinhey, ECG. *Moths of Southern Africa*. Tafelberg: Cape Town, 1975
Punt, Dr WHJ. *The First Europeans in the Kruger National Park*. Simon v.d. Stel
   Foundation: Pretoria, 1975

Reeder, J & Crozer, H. *Pyramids of Life*. Collins: Johannesburg, 1977

Reitz, Denys. *Commando*. Faber & Faber: London, 1929

Roberts' Birds of South Africa. 4th ed. Struik: Cape Town, 1977

Skaife, SH. *African Insect Life*. Struik: Cape Town, 1979

Smithers Reay HN. *The Mammals of the South African Subregion*. University of Pretoria: Pretoria, 1983

Stevenson-Hamilton, J. *The Lowveld: Its Wild Life & Its People*. Cassell & Co: London, 1929

South African Eden. Cassell & Co: London, 1937

Taylor, JB. *A Pioneer Looks Back*. Hutchinson: London, 1939

Voigt. *50 Years of the History of the Republic of South Africa 1795-1845, Vol I*. Struik: Cape Town, 1969

Wilson, M & Thompson L (eds). *The Oxford History of the Republic of South Africa, Vol I and II*. Oxford University Press: Oxford, 1969

LEGEND

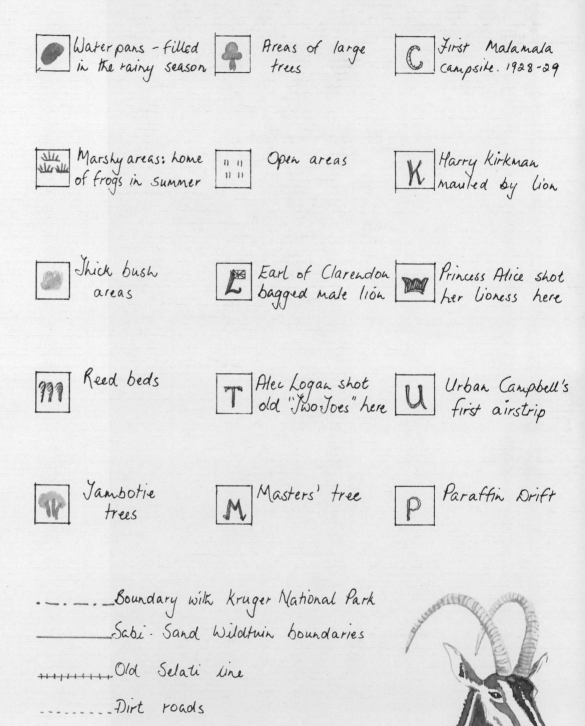

Waterpans – filled in the rainy season	Areas of large trees	**C** First Malamala campsite. 1928-29
Marshy areas: home of frogs in summer	Open areas	**K** Harry Kirkman mauled by lion
Thick bush areas	**E** Earl of Clarendon bagged male lion	Princess Alice shot her lioness here
m Reed beds	**T** Alec Logan shot old "TwoToes" here	**U** Urban Campbell's first airstrip
Tambotie trees	**M** Masters' tree	**P** Paraffin Drift

–·–·–·–·– Boundary with Kruger National Park

————— Sabi-Sand Wildtuin boundaries

++++++++ Old Selati line

- - - - - - - - Dirt roads